HARMONIC RELATIONS

A practical textbook for the study
of Harmony

by

CARL McKINLEY

Revised Edition

RESOURCE *Publications* · Eugene, Oregon

Resource Publications
A division of Wipf and Stock Publishers
199 W 8th Ave, Suite 3
Eugene, OR 97401

Harmonic Relations
A Practical Textbook for the Study of Harmony
By McKinley, Carl
ISBN 13: 978-1-61097-531-5
Publication date 5/6/2011
Previously published by New England Conservatory of Music, 1944

CONTENTS

INTRODUCTORY NOTE

to the

REVISED EDITION

Since its first appearance in 1938 "Harmonic Relations" has been in continuous use in the classrooms of the New England Conservatory of Music. Every chapter, illustration and exercise has been subjected to the most careful scrutiny, in an effort to make each statement and explanation as simple and clear as possible, and the exercise material varied, musical and attractive.

The revised edition has benefited greatly from the combined experience of students and teaching staff. Material that proved of doubtful value has been eliminated, the order of presentation has been considerably revised, and much new material has been added, particularly in the latter part of the book. Its principal object is to provide the student with a comprehensive knowledge of the principles of harmonic writing as they may be observed in the works of the great composers of the past, and a theoretical basis for the investigation of the divergent harmonic practices of contemporary writers.

Extensive analysis of the standard literature is of the utmost importance, and should parallel the theoretical work. Short quotations from well-known composers have been entirely omitted from the present book, as such excerpts, divorced from their context, seldom give a clear impression of the effect intended. Instead there is provided a separate volume of "Examples for Harmonic Analysis" covering a wide range of music from the beginnings of harmony down to the twentieth century, and containing copious illustrations of all the harmonic problems discussed in the text book.

The author acknowledges most gratefully the many helpful suggestions of Quincy Porter, Director of the New England Conservatory of Music, without whose cooperation the present volume could not have been issued; many valuable ideas have been contributed by his colleagues in the theory department, and special thanks are due Francis Judd Cooke for his assistance in the preparation of the manuscript.

BOSTON, MASSACHUSETTS
NOVEMBER 24, 1943

CHAPTER I

SCALES

1 **Harmonic relations** are present in nearly all music, no matter how simple. The study of these relations includes the analysis of the intervallic structure of various simultaneous sound combinations called chords, and of the various ways in which they may be connected, called chord progression. Standard theoretical procedure up to the end of the nineteenth century recognized as chords only those sound combinations produced by erecting three or more tones upon a given fundamental in a series of thirds, and considered all other tones to be "non-harmonic". Contemporary practice, recognizing the limitations of this system, accepts any possible combination of the twelve tones of the chromatic scale as a chord, whose definite place in a scale of values may be readily determined.

2 **The Harmonic Series.** The basic material of any musical system is a series of musical tones from which the chords are constructed, and in order to express any logical musical thought this series must have definite and fixed inter-relationships. Such a series exists in the *harmonic series* of partials or overtones sometimes called the "chord of nature".

Ex. 1

3 **The Diatonic Major Scale.** The *harmonic series* is melodically unsatisfactory, however, as its most audible portion progresses by rather wide and unmelodic leaps; for practical purposes the tones of a system are more conveniently arranged in scalewise order, proceeding by step. The historical evolution of our *diatonic major scale* and its various derivatives, is far too long and complicated to be introduced here; but the practical nature of this universal scale may be easily demonstrated. In the harmonic series shown in Ex. 1 it may be noted that since the second partial is merely the octave repetition of the fundamental tone, *the third partial* (G in the series of C) *is the nearest related overtone* that is not a repetition of the fundamental at a different octave. This is the physical basis for the *dominant* relationship of the interval of the fifth in all musical systems which are based upon a tonal "center of gravity" called the *tonic* or key-tone, occupying a position of higher value and importance than any other tone in the scale. The two tones most closely related to any given tonic, such as C in the illustration, are those related to it by the interval of a fifth, of which there are two, the *dominant* or fifth *above*, and the *subdominant* or fifth *below*. By taking the harmonic series of these three tones we find that all the tones of the major scale are present as closely related overtones in one of the three series, and several in more than one.

Ex. 2

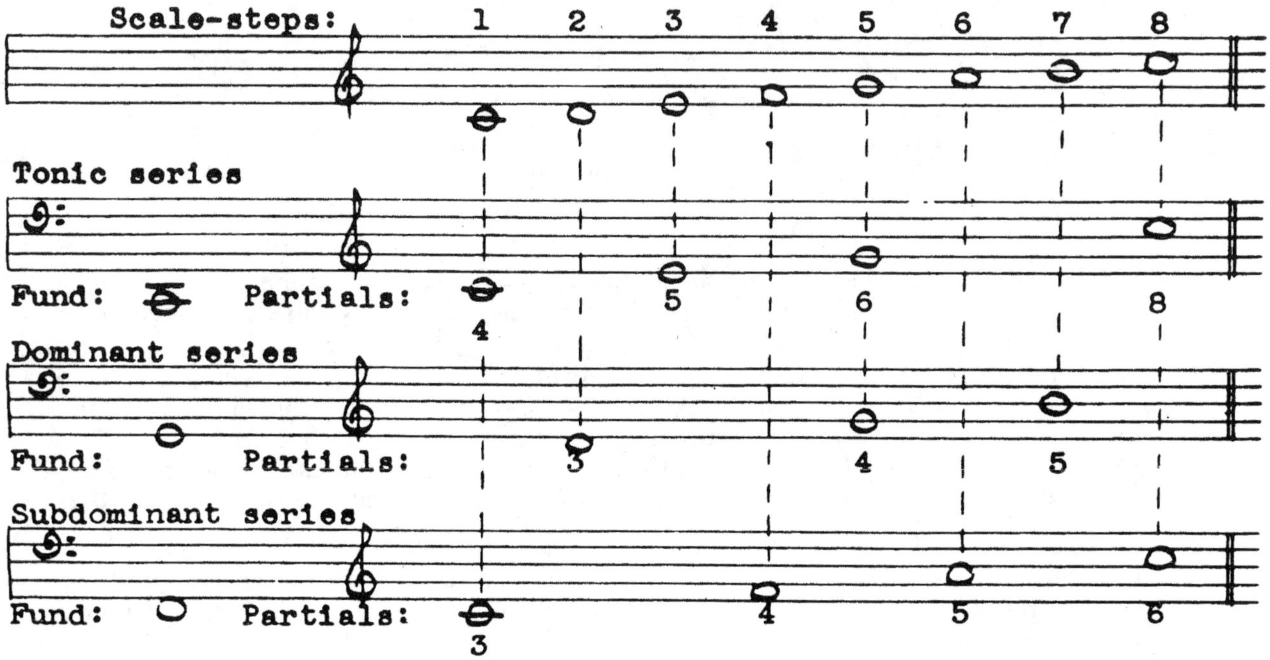

In the practical application of this scale, particularly to keyboard instruments, certain adjustments in tuning called equal temperament are necessary, so that of all the intervals only the octave is pure. The small loss in auditory pleasure is more than compensated for by the immense gain in adaptability to all kinds of harmonic procedure.

Thus derived, *the diatonic major scale is a series of seven tones within the octave proceeding stepwise by whole steps except between the third and fourth, and the seventh and eighth, which are half steps.*

4 **The Chromatic Scale**, proceeding exclusively by half steps, has generally been thought of as a derivative or amplification of the diatonic major scale, and it was so considered by most composers up to the beginning of the twentieth century. Contemporary practice stresses the importance of viewing the chromatic tones as independent entities, and not as derivatives, observing that their relationship to the fundamental tonic is more distant. Paul Hindemith, in his *"Craft of Musical Composition"* (Associated Music Publishers, N. Y.) Part I, p. 32 ff, demonstrates these relationships through coincidences in the partials of the various tones.

5 **The Tritone.** The one chromatic tone whose relationship cannot be clearly demonstrated in this way is the one that theoretically divides the scale exactly in half: F sharp, or its *enharmonic,* G flat, in the scale of C.* The interval of the *tritone* (three whole tones) which it forms with the fundamental, C, plays a highly important role in all problems of tonality, precisely because of its ambiguity which causes the ear to seek other relationships for its explanation. Tritones are to be found in the *harmonic series*: the one between the fifth and seventh partials is very small, that between the seventh and tenth large, and between the eighth and eleventh partials, again smaller. The augmented fourth is thus a very artificial interval which may vary greatly in size under different circumstances.

*For purposes of simplicity in the present discussion, tones represented by *enharmonic* notation, such as C sharp and D flat, will be considered to be the same tone. At the same time, the difference in pitch should not be lost sight of, as it is a real one in vocal music and that produced from instruments of variable pitch, and a psychological one where the sounds come from a keyboard instrument; although produced by depressing the same key on the piano or organ, we undoubtedly *hear* F sharp as higher in pitch than G flat.

6 **The Relative Minor Scale** is a derivative of the diatonic major scale, beginning upon the latter's sixth degree. It is called *relative* because of the fact that it uses the same key signature, and also because of the facility with which it reverts or *modulates* back to the original major form. In its natural form this scale is a survival of the Gregorian Mode known as Aeolian. It progresses by whole steps except between the second and third, and the fifth and sixth, which are half steps. In practical use it normally undergoes some chromatic alteration, which will be discussed in the proper place.

7 **Key.** A complete diatonic or chromatic scale may commence upon any of the twelve fundamental tones which exist between C and its octave. Thus are derived the fifteen keys of the classical system, three of which are enharmonic duplicates:

C	G	D	A	E	B	F#	C#				
					Cb	Gb	Db	Ab	Eb	Bb	F
1	2	3	4	5	6	7	8	9	10	11	12

For purposes of distinction between these different keys, the diatonic scale is obviously much better adapted than the chromatic, for in the diatonic scale the two semitone progressions will be represented by new tones for each new tonic, or key-tone. Even in very chromatic writing a feeling of tonal center may be maintained by the frequent repetition of tones closely related to it, or by the selection of a certain group of chromatic tones and the avoidance of others. The great bulk of established musical masterworks, however, have been written in the diatonic system, in which the chromatic tones were regarded as accessories, often highly important as "neighbor" tones, but still having a lower scale of harmonic values than the fundamental tones of the major scale.

Exercise 1. Write the diatonic major scales of the seven sharp keys and the seven flat keys in both treble and bass clefs. Do not use a signature, but place the necessary accidentals in the proper places in each scale. *After* you have completed this, write the signature in the proper place, being sure that the signs are correctly placed.

Exercise 2. Write the chromatic scales, both ascending and descending, beginning on D, E flat, F sharp and C flat. Alternate treble and bass clefs, and use the signatures of the corresponding major keys. In ascending, use sharps or cancels, in descending, cancels or flats, and where necessary, double sharps and double flats.

CHAPTER II

INTERVALS

1 **Definition.** The unit of harmonic structure is the *interval,* which may be defined as the distance between two tones of different pitch, sounded either together or in direct succession. When sounded together an *harmonic interval* is formed; when in succession, a *melodic interval.* Intervals are referred to by a number which represents the sum of the letters involved; the interval from C to F above is a fourth, C, D, E, F. Accidentals may be applied to one or both tones of an interval without changing its number name.

2 **Classification of intervals.** The keytone of a given diatonic major scale makes seven different intervallic combinations with the other tones of the scale above it. Of these the fourth, fifth and octave are called *perfect,** and the second, third, sixth and seventh, *major.* The unison or prime, also called *perfect,* is not in itself an interval, but may become one through chromatic alteration of one of its tones.

Utilizing the chromatic tones, there are twelve possible intervallic combinations, *in sound,* within the octave, and through enharmonic spelling several more become available. In order of diminishing size they are as follows:

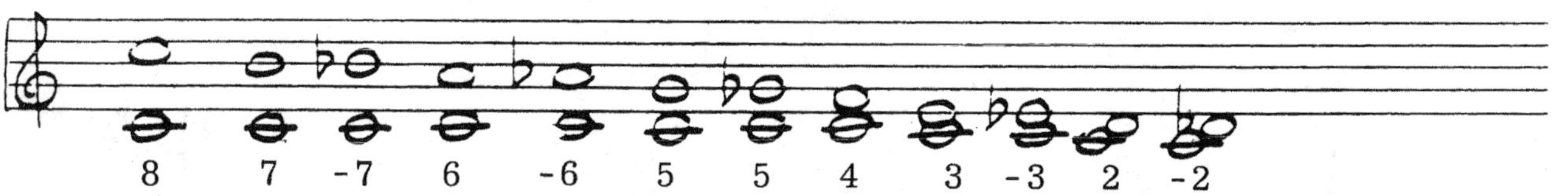

It will be seen that the sevenths, sixths, thirds and seconds all have a larger and a smaller form, to which the terms *major* and *minor* are applied. It is convenient to designate minor intervals by placing a minus sign before the appropriate figure. The smaller form of the fifth, C to G flat, forming the important interval of the *tritone,* is called a *diminished* fifth, and indicated by a small circle at the left of the number. These twelve intervals are the only ones (based upon the same lower tone) that can be distinguished *in sound,* unless placed in a context where they are heard not as reduced forms of major or perfect intervals, but as enlarged or augmented forms of these intervals. In notation, however, several enharmonic forms are available; an enharmonic change in the minor second gives us the *augmented* prime. Other augmented intervals, indicated by a plus sign before the number, are as follows:

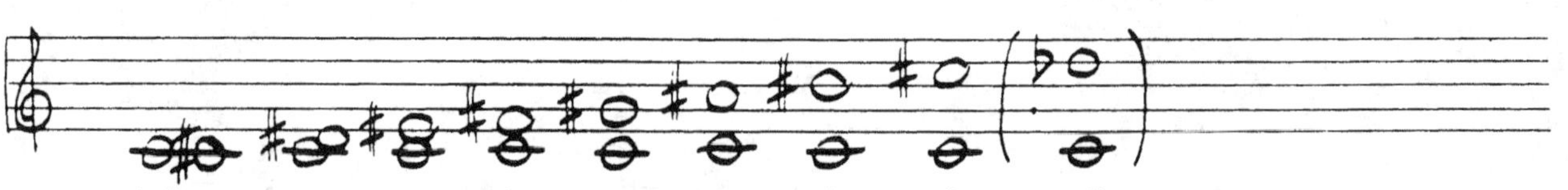

* The term "perfect" was used by early theorists to distinguish between the so-called "perfect" concords: fourth, fifth and octave, and the "imperfect" concords: major and minor thirds and sixths. It probably refers to the fact that the perfect concords are theoretically uniform in size, while the imperfect concords, even in an untempered scale, vary considerably according to their position in that scale.

Both major and minor ninths, especially when they occur in the so-called ninth chords, should be distinguished from their simpler original forms, the major and minor second. An octave is usually deducted from all larger intervals, the tenth being considered the same as a third, etc.

Any of the perfect intervals become diminished if their size is reduced by a semitone. A similar process may be applied to minor intervals, but only the diminished seventh and the diminished third are of frequent occurrence. At least one well-known chord is built around the interval of the *doubly augmented fourth.* While other doubly augmented and doubly diminished intervals may be constructed, their value is largely theoretical.

3 **Measurement of intervals.** The sizes of the various intervals measured from the keynote upwards provide us with absolute criteria for the measurement of all other intervals, no matter where they begin. The size of any interval may be readily determined by comparing it with the corresponding interval of the major scale of its lower tone. The wider intervals are conveniently measured by subdivision; thus a perfect fifth is the sum of a major and minor third, a perfect fourth is a semitone larger than a major third, a minor sixth is a minor third added to a perfect fourth, etc.

TABLE OF INTERVALS

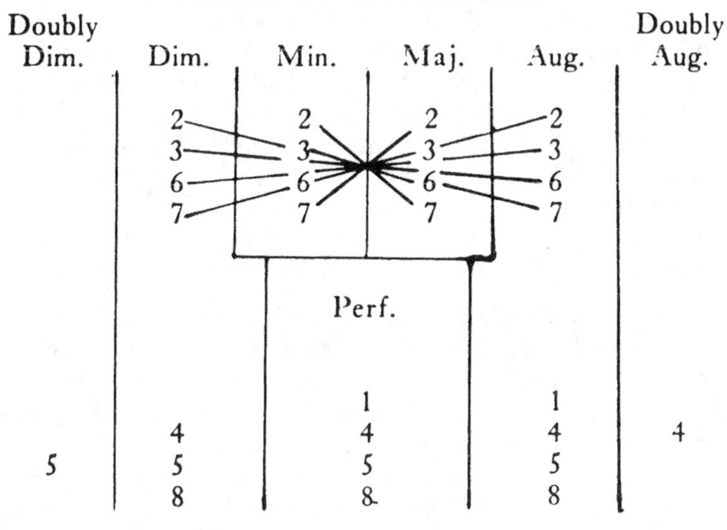

Moving one column to the right increases the size of the interval by a semitone.

4 **Inversion of intervals.** The rearrangement of any given interval by placing the lower tone an octave higher produces its *inversion.* The pattern for this procedure is found in the harmonic series, where the fifth, C to G (partials 2 and 3) becomes the fourth, G to C (partials 3 and 4). Note that the fundamental tone of both intervals is C. The inversions of the more common intervals are shown in the following table. Observe that

Perfect intervals inverted remain perfect.
Major intervals inverted become minor, and vice versa.
Augmented intervals inverted become diminished, and vice versa.
The sum of an interval and its inversion is always nine; (6 + 3 = 9, etc.)

INVERSION OF INTERVALS

5 **Harmonic value of intervals.** The harmonic value of an interval is determined by its stability as an independent harmonic unit. The most stable interval, and the one having the *highest* harmonic value, is the octave; at the other end of the scale of values is the minor second, with its strongly active tendency, which is the most unstable, and therefore has the *lowest* harmonic value. The arrangement of the remaining intervals between these two is determined by various factors, of which the simplicity of ratio, as expressed in the harmonic series, is undoubtedly the most important. Thus the intervals may be arranged in an order of diminishing values by passing from the simplest (the octave, 1::2) to the most complex, (the minor second, 17::18). The order is easily determined until one reaches the so-called "dissonant" intervals, (sevenths, seconds, tritone) where owing to the large differences of intonation in active or tendency tones, the exact ratio is often difficult to determine.

The question of consonance and dissonance is also to be considered in determining the harmonic value of an interval. These terms are difficult to define, as they change in their meaning according to the period and style of the music under consideration. In early harmonic history thirds were considered too dissonant to be used in final chords, while today major seconds and minor seconds have almost acquired the status of consonances. Beats occur as often as the vibrations of two tones strike a like phase. When these beats are audible they give the effect of dissonance. The standard classification, to which we will adhere for purposes of analysis, considers all seconds, sevenths and the tritone as having sufficiently audible beats to make them dissonant, as well as all augmented and diminished intervals, even though some of the latter are identical on keyboard instruments with consonant intervals. (Thus the intervals C to G sharp and C to A flat are the same on the pianoforte.)

Another important factor in the determination of harmonic values is the conflict of prominent overtones. It will be seen from the table below that these tend to confirm the arrangement according to ratios. Thus the "dissonant" quality of the fourth under many circumstances may be traced to the conflict between the third partial of the lower tone and the second partial of the upper. It will be noticed, however, that the semitone conflict occurs between the third partial of the lower tone and the second partial of the upper in both the minor sixth and the augmented fourth, though there is a great difference in their ratios, and it becomes apparent that the more complicated the ratio, the less important is the conflict of overtones as a factor in producing the impression of relative dissonance.

In fact, the proportionate amount of upper partials in the tone of different instruments varies so greatly that certain intervals sound (and actually are) more dissonant on some instruments than on others. A perfect fourth may sound quite smooth from two French horns which develop relatively few overtones, and yet clash sharply if played by instruments rich in upper partials such as the oboe or clarinet. Thus the conflict of overtones is seen to be a variable factor, while the simplicity of ratio is a much more constant and dependable one.

In the following table the intervals on the lower line are arranged in order of diminishing harmonic value, as determined by their ratios, which are shown in figures between the lines. On the upper line are the partials of the two tones in each interval, some of the more prominent conflicts being indicated by diagonal lines.

HARMONIC VALUE OF INTERVALS

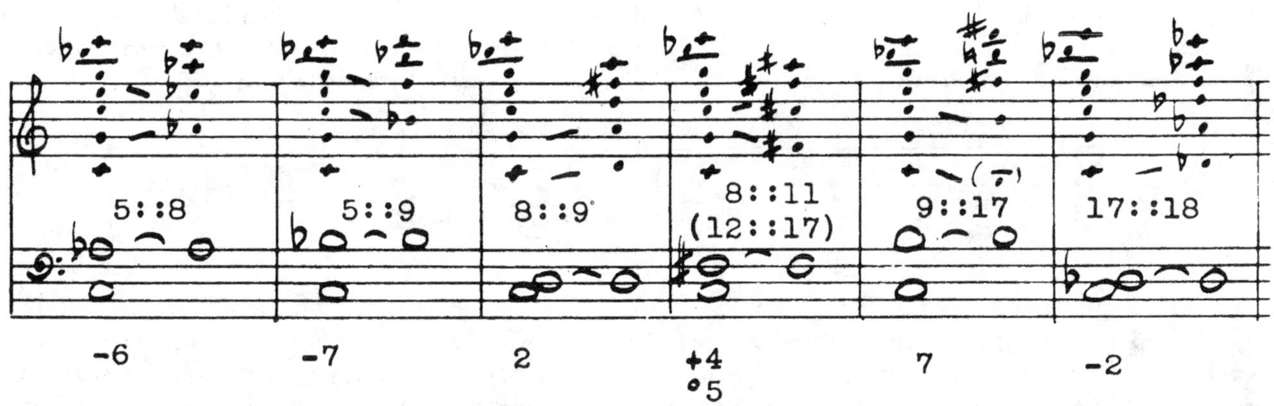

Exercise: Write out the intervals in the table of intervals on page 9 in notation, making the lower tone C in each case. Be sure to indicate each interval with the proper sign. (Numbers without signs are perfect or major intervals).

CHAPTER III

TRIADS; TONALITY

Chords. A chord is a group of three or more different tones sounded together. There is some reason for believing that in the earliest harmonic experiments of composers before the fifteenth century, the perfect fourth rather than the "imperfect" third was the unit of chord structure. However, the great schools of classical composition were based exclusively on chords consisting of two or three superimposed thirds, the lowest tone being considered the *root,* or fundamental tone of the chord. Chords erected by thirds which do not exceed the octave are readily invertible; that is, their root tone may appear in an upper voice and not in the bass without destroying the identity of the chord. Chords which exceed the interval of an octave, such as ninth chords, are inverted only with difficulty; and chords containing seconds and fourths above the root as essential intervals are not in any real sense invertible at all.

2 **Triads.** The simplest of all chords is the *triad,* consisting of three tones, a fundamental tone called the root,, and two others lying respectively a third and a fifth above it. The purest form of triad is to be observed in the harmonic-series between partials 4, 5 and 6. This consists of a root, a major third and a perfect fifth, and is called a *major triad.* Observe that the quality of a chord is determined by the relationship of its various tones to the root. The triads erected upon the fourth and fifth degrees of the major scale are similarly constituted to that upon the first degree. As already noted, these three triads, the Tonic, Subdominant and Dominant, which may be conveniently represented by the Roman numerals I, IV and V, contain all the tones of the major scale, and their fundamental importance is such that they are designated *Primary Triads.*

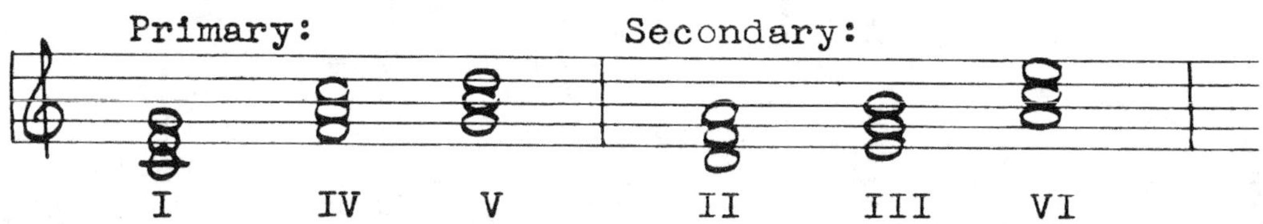

The triads on II, III and VI, called respectively the Supertonic, the Mediant (halfway between Tonic and Dominant) and the Submediant, (halfway between Tonic and Subdominant) are of lesser harmonic importance, and are termed *Secondary Triads.* It will be observed that they consist of a *minor* third and perfect fifth above the root, and their quality is minor; hence the term *minor triad.* The general effect of the major triads is usually described as bright, serene or energetic; of the minor as dull, sad, pathetic.

3 **Dissonant Triads.** The seventh scale-step of the major scale, because of its strong melodic tendency towards the keytone or Tonic, is called the Leading Tone. The triad upon it contains the dissonant interval of the diminished fifth (tritone). The result is a *diminished triad,* consisting of minor third and diminished fifth, which is so active and unstable harmonically as to require special treatment, called *resolution.* The Leading Tone, because of its active quality, which is greatly intensified by the simultaneous sounding of the diminished fifth above it, can hardly be considered as a fundamental tone of any chord, and it should be noted that there is available *no root triad* upon the seventh degree of the major scale. The seventh degree of the natural minor scale is a whole step below the Tonic, and to distinguish these two tones and the chords upon them we will reserve the figure VII and the term Subtonic for the minor scale, and refer to the *leading tone triad* of major keys by the letter L.

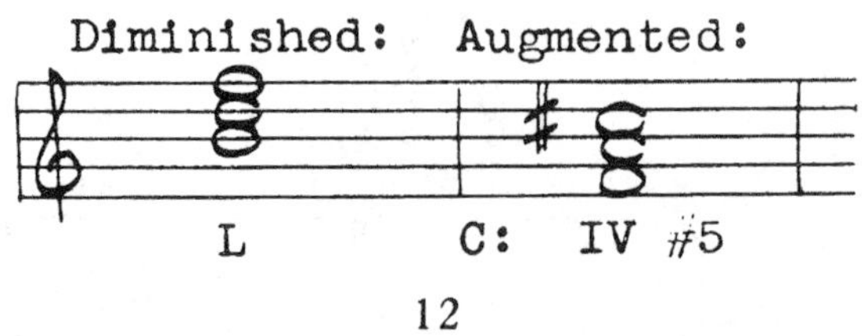

The *augmented triad,* consisting of major third and augmented fifth, does not occur in the unaltered major or minor scales, but has to be artificially produced by augmenting the fifth of a major triad. By itself this triad is curiously vague and ambiguous. Like the diminished triad it contains two equal intervals, but altogether lacks the sharp tonal definition of the diminished fifth, which makes every diminished triad sound like a leading tone triad. A major third sets up a strong feeling that the lower tone is its fundamental, and as the chord contains two major thirds there is a struggle between them for supremacy; while the interval of the augmented fifth by itself is indistinguishable from the minor sixth, whose fundamental tone is its upper one, (harmonic series, partials 5 and 8). Thus any of its tones might serve as root, and it is really uninvertible, the apparent "inversions" merely producing a rise in pitch without any actual change in the quality of the chord.

4 **Tonality.** The principles of *tonality* govern the harmonic and formal structure of music in a way somewhat analogous to that in which perspective governs the arrangement and design of a drawing or painting. Comparison of an art existing in time with one existing in space is always dangerous, the only point of contact between tonality and perspective being that both exert a force which tends to bring order out of chaos. By *tonality* is meant the selection of one tone in a scale and the triad based upon it as the central point of a system, around which the other tones and their chords are arranged in a definite order of receding importance. The treatment and arrangement of these chords all tends to confirm the tonic as the central point and fundamental of the whole system, in which the two *dominants,* from above and below, play a vital role. The upward pull of the dominant above, (V) is counteracted by the downward pull of the subdominant, (IV), which exerts an equal force in maintaining tonal stability. Schoenberg, in his "Harmonielehre" makes a picturesque comparison of the forces involved to the strength of a man who is hanging by his arms from a beam and who thereby counteracts with the strength of his body the force of gravity. He pulls in the same direction on the beam as gravity pulls on him. The result is such that his power works against gravity, warranting the representation of the two powers as working against each other.

The vital importance of the *dominant triad* upon tonal feeling is due not only to its being built upon the third partial of the tonic as root, but still more to the fact that its third is the *leading tone,* with its intense upward melodic activity. This feeling is so strong that the mere sounding of the leading tone, sometimes as a note of very short duration, is quite sufficient to establish the feeling of complete dominant harmony.

The *subdominant triad* supplies the two scale tones not found in the combined tones of the tonic and dominant triads, (scale-steps 4 and 6), so that the three primary chords sound all the tones of the scale. Among the secondary triads, the *supertonic* also contains the fourth and sixth scale-steps, and may be used as an alternate for the subdominant; it therefore has greater tonal value than any of the other secondary triads; of these, the *submediant* is frequently used as an alternate for the tonic, and the *mediant* may be used as an alternate for the dominant, as it contains the essential leading tone. However it contains the thirds of *both* tonic and dominant triads, and is so evenly balanced between them, and therefore so ambiguous tonally, that its use is rather infrequent.

The diminishing order of tonal value of the triads is as follows:

I, V, IV, II, VI, III.

5 **Formation of chords from triads.** Our present harmonic system is most conveniently studied on the basis of a four part vocal score. The individual parts should not exceed the natural compass of the four singing voices, soprano, alto, tenor and bass. Do not write leger lines either above the treble staff or below the bass.

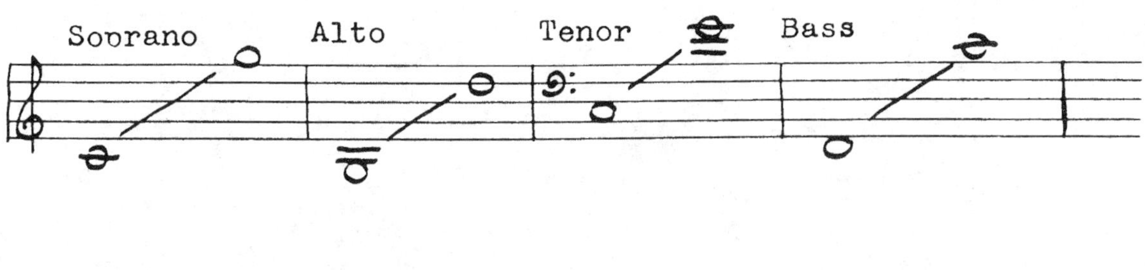

Doubling. It is obvious that in providing a note for each of the four voices in a four part score, some note of each triad will have to be doubled. The rules of doubling cannot be fully formulated until all the elementary harmonic material has been presented. For the present, the various possibilities will be taken up one at a time. *The strongest harmonic doubling is the root,* and the first exercises will be concerned exclusively with *root doubling.*

Spacing. The other problem involved in making four note chords from triads is that of spacing. While exceptions will be met later on, the general rule may be stated as follows:

The Rule of Spacing:

The note given to the alto part should never be more than an octave from the soprano or the tenor part.

Exercise: Following the model given below, form as many four note chords as possible from the I, IV and V triads in the keys assigned by the instructor. Take care not to exceed the natural compass of the four voices, and to observe the rule of spacing. Double only the root. When the upper *three* notes of a chord lie within the compass of an octave, the chord is said to be in "close" position. Otherwise it is in "open" position. The figures above the chords indicate which note of the triad is in the soprano. If it is the third, the chord is said to be in the *position of the third,* etc.

CHAPTER IV

CHORD-ROOT PROGRESSIONS IN CLASS I

1 **Underlying Principles.** Satisfactory chord connection is only obtained through a careful study of the principles underlying the progression of chord-roots. For convenience, we will divide the study of these progressions into three groups, depending upon the relationships between the roots themselves, as expressed in the *harmonic series.*

The most closely related tones in this series are those at the interval of a perfect fifth, and its inversion the perfect fourth. We will therefore designate all chord progressions in which the roots move a fifth or fourth as *Class I* progressions.

Between the fourth, fifth, and sixth harmonics we find the interval of a major or minor third. Progressions of chord-roots which move a third, therefore, are designated *Class II* progressions.

Above the eighth partial the interval between harmonics is a major second or smaller. As shown in the table of harmonic value of intervals, p. 11 these intervals have the smallest harmonic value, and all stepwise progressions of chord-roots belong in *Class III.*

Since the inversion of a sixth is a third, and of a seventh a second, all possible movements of chord-roots are covered in the above classification, and the widest permissible leap between chord-roots is a perfect fifth.

2 **Class I progressions.** All triads whose roots lie a fourth or a fifth apart have one tone which occurs in both of them and which is therefore called a *common tone.* If convenient, the common tone may be kept in the same part, but this is often impossible. The procedure is as follows:

a) *If the common tone is kept* in the same part, the bass will move from root to root, and the other parts *stepwise.*

b) *If the common tone is not kept* in the same part, the *rule of contrary motion applies;* it may be simply formulated as follows:

The Rule of Contrary Motion: *Move the upper three parts in contrary motion to the bass.*

Exercise 1. Following the model below, write the progressions I - V - I, and I - IV - I in various keys, as assigned by the instructor.

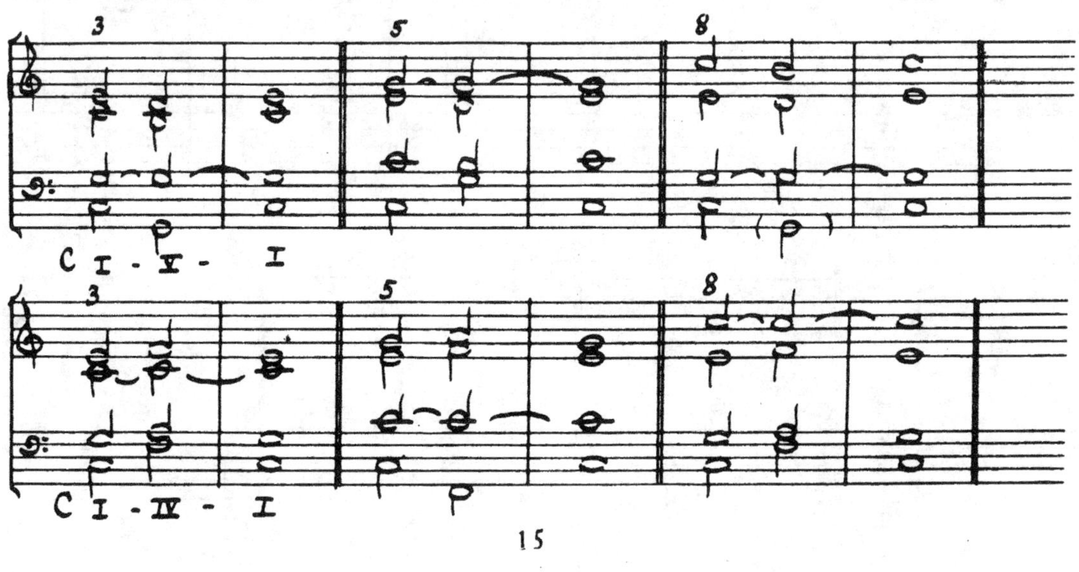

Exercise 2. Reproduce the following model in several keys, as assigned.

3 **Progressive and regressive order.** A feeling of progress or movement towards a goal results from those progressions in which the root of the second chord is a new tone, not sounded in the first chord. In Class I, those roots which *fall a fifth* fulfill this requirement, while those which *fall a fourth* do not. We will therefore call the former *progressive,* and the latter *regressive* movements. Beginning with the *mediant,* which is the root of the chord farthest removed from the key-center, we get the following series of roots in progressive order:

Since a rising fourth reaches the octave of the same tone as a falling fifth, we may express the same series equally well by a succession of alternate fourths and fifths, with the advantage of a more compact range. Observe that no perfect fifth below or perfect fourth above the subdominant root is available, and IV is therefore compelled to return to I, thus confirming it as tonic.

Exercise 3. Reproduce the following model in various keys, as assigned.

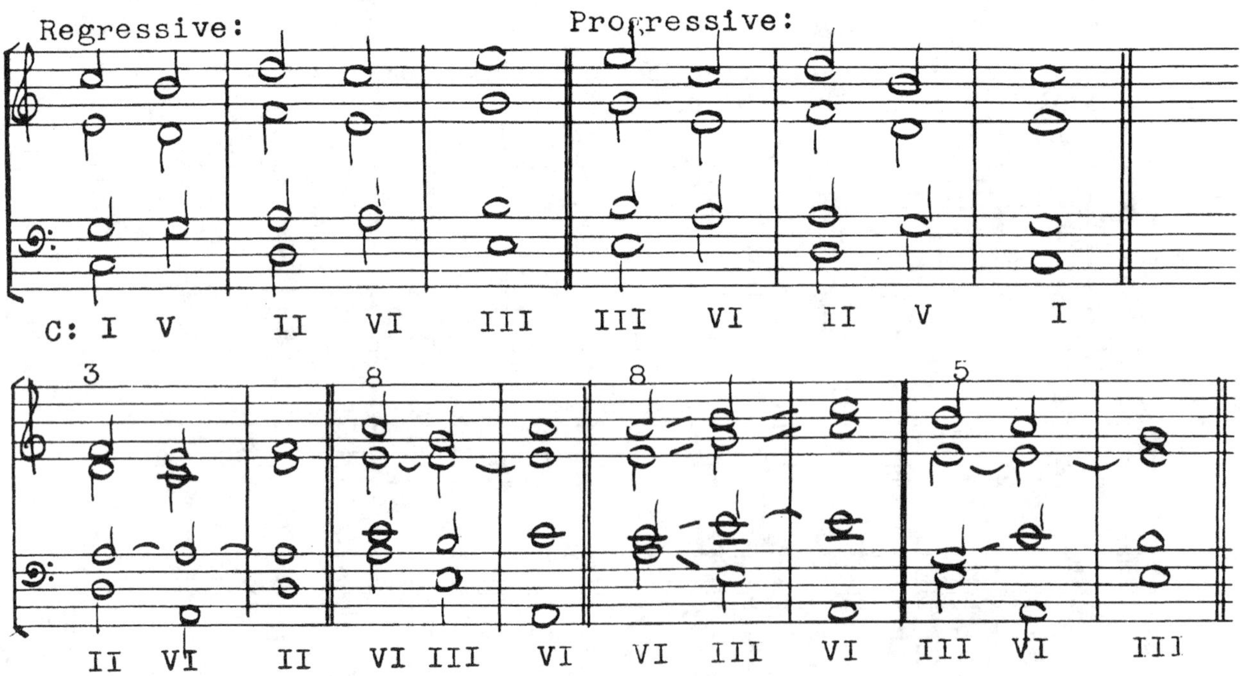

Note: With scalewise melody, the common tone may be kept if a change is made from open to close position, or vice versa, as in the last example above. The tenor and soprano parts of this illustration could be reversed so that the fourth skip occurs in the soprano. The skip must always be made *upwards* from the *third* of the first chord.

Keyboard Exercise; Write out all the three note melodies you can think of within the soprano range in the key of C according to the following formulas:

a) stepwise up and back
b) stepwise down and back
c) scalewise up
d) scalewise down
e) skip down third and return stepwise
f) skip up fourth and return stepwise

With these melodies in front of you, harmonize them in Class I at the keyboard. If necessary, the bass part may also be written out for the first trials. Later, reverse the process, having in front of you only the written bass part, with Roman numerals.

CHAPTER V

CHORD-ROOT PROGRESSIONS IN CLASS II

1 The progressive order of chord-roots in Class II is *downward*. Because the leading tone is not available as a root, the series is broken into two parts:

Observe that in all Class II progressions there are two common tones. The effect, therefore, is one of similarity rather than of contrast, and chords based upon alternate degrees of the scale are frequently used as alternates or substitutes for each other.

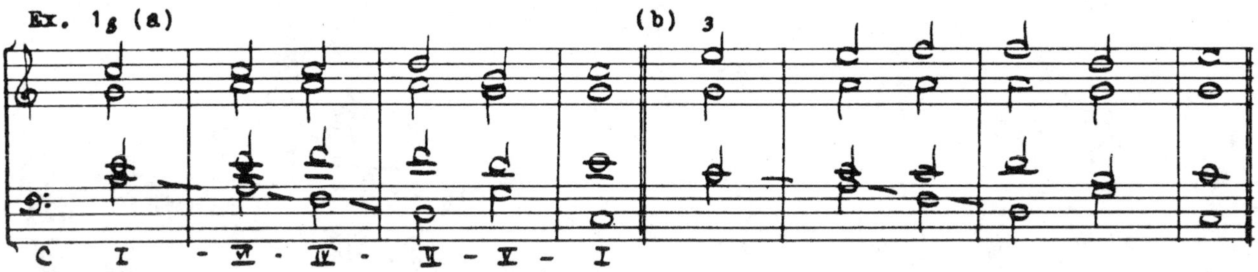

In Class II progressions it is usually best to keep the *two common tones in the same voices.* If this is not done, the *rule of contrary motion* always applies. Failure to observe this rule will almost certainly result in a violation of the *rule of consecutives,* which may be formulated as follows:

The Rule of Consecutives:

Consecutive fifths or octaves by either parallel or contrary motion are forbidden.

The regressive order in Class II is very weak; however it may be used in such progressions as I - VI - I, or V - III - V, where the middle chord is in effect an "embellishing" chord. In each case the first and third chords must be the same, and the effect is best when the fifth of the first chord is in the soprano.

Embellishing Chords

Note: The leap of a sixth between chord-roots in Class II is strictly forbidden.

Exercise. Reproduce in the keys assigned by the instructor the chord progressions given in Example 1 above.

Keyboard Exercise. 1. Play all the progressions in Class II that are available to harmonize a ***repeated melody note*** in the scale of C. Try all the scale tones, noting which of them have two different patterns, (C-C may be harmonized with I - VI or VI - IV), which of them has only one pattern, and which has none at all.

2. Find and play the Class II progression that harmonizes each pair of tones in the scale of C moving *stepwise up*, (C-D, D-E, etc.)

3. Do the same for each possible ***upward fourth-leap*** in the scale of C. (C-F, D-G, etc.)

4. Repeat the above in such other keys as are assigned by the instructor.

CHAPTER VI

CHORD-ROOT PROGRESSIONS IN CLASS III

1 Since there are no common tones in these progressions, the root of the second chord is always a new tone. The question of progressive and regressive order is determined in this case by the ***diminishing order of tonal value*** of the triads, as described on p. 13. Thus the progression I - II - III is regressive; III - IV - V returns towards the key center, and V - VI is again regressive.

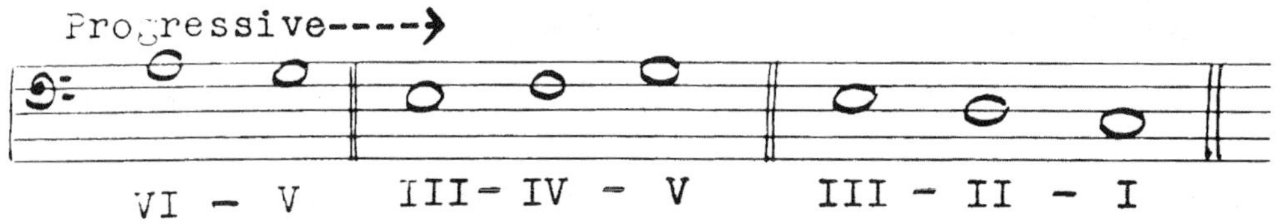

2 The most common Class III progression is that of the subdominant into the dominant. As no common tones are present, the *rule of contrary motion always applies*. The roots move upwards, the upper three parts will all move downwards, Ex. 1.

Ex. 1

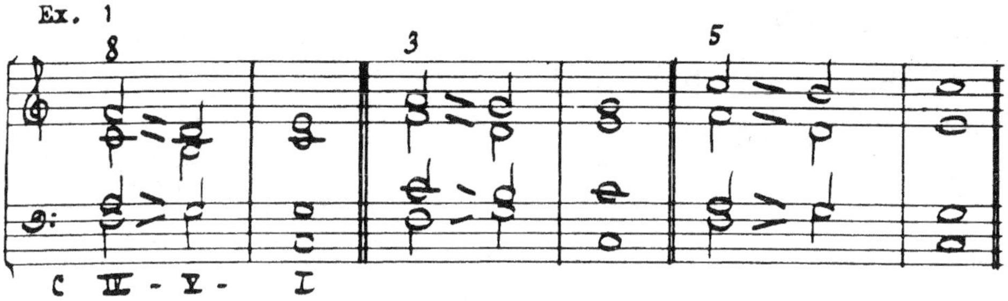

3 If the *rule of contrary motion* is not observed, "hidden" fifths or octaves are very likely to result. These are the result of similar (but not parallel) motion to a fifth or an octave, and are only objectionable when they occur in the *outside* voices, (soprano and bass). The *rule of similar motion* may be formulated as follows:

The Rule of Similar Motion:

Similar motion between outside voices is always good if the second interval is a third or sixth. If it is a fifth or octave, however, it may only be used when the upper voice moves by step.

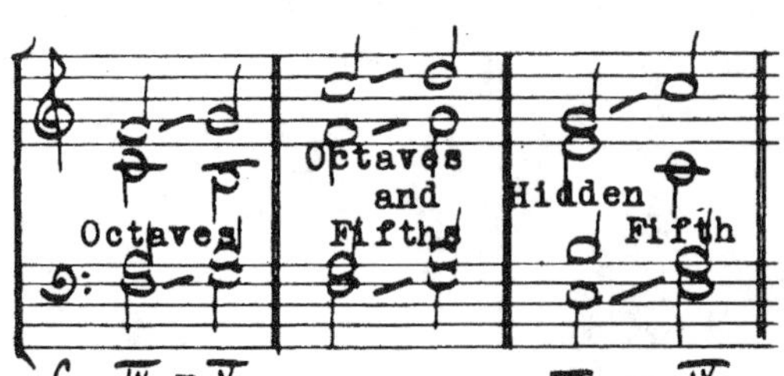

4 The progression V-VI is also very common, and since it interrupts the normal tendency of V to I it may be called a *deceptive progression.* The *leading tone,* in the first of these two chords, usually follows its strong natural tendency to resolve stepwise upwards, even though this results in a doubled *third* in the submediant chord. The parallel motion, it should be noted, is in thirds, and the second third is minor, Ex. 3. The same treatment may be applied to the progression I-II, Ex. 4. These are the only possible exceptions to the *rule of contrary motion,* in Class III; it is followed in all other progressions such as that in Ex. 5, where, since the roots move downwards, the upper three parts move up.

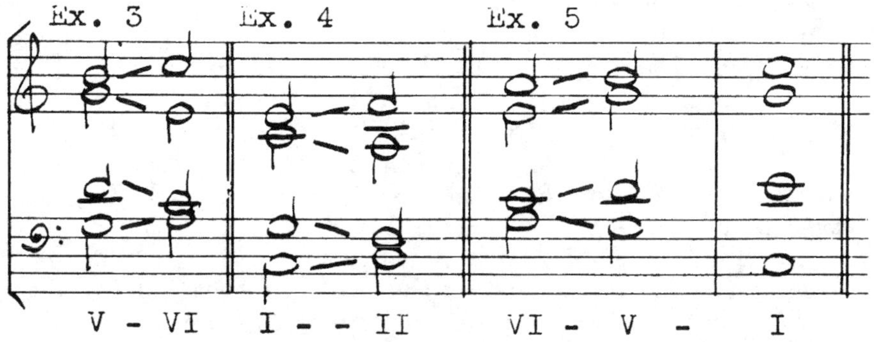

5 The mediant triad is frequently used to harmonize the leading tone when it occurs in a melody *descending scalewise,* Ex. 6. The use of embellishing chords in Class III is frequent; in every case the first and third chords, which precede and follow the embellishing chord, must be identical, Ex. 7.

Note: The leap of a seventh between chord-roots in Class III is strictly forbidden.

Exercise: Reproduce the following chord progressions in various keys, as assigned:

1. I — IV — V — I
2. I — II — V — I
3. I — III — IV — V — I
4. I — V — VI — II — V — I
5. I — II — III — VI — V — I

Keyboard Exercise:

1. Find and play the Class III progressions that harmonize each pair of tones in the scale of C moving *stepwise down.*
2. Do the same for each pair of tones moving *stepwise up.*
3. Do the same for each possible *downward leap of a third.*
4. Repeat the above in such other keys as are assigned.

CHAPTER VII

HARMONIZATION OF MELODIES

1 **Phrases.** Simple melodies may be readily harmonized with root triads, affording practice in realizing the implied harmony of any given melodic tone. The tones of even the simplest melody group themselves into *phrases,* which are indicated by slurs above the melodic line. A very short melody may consist of only one continuous phrase, but usually there are two or more. A slur does not necessarily determine the extent of a phrase, for at times it merely indicates the articulation of a repeated tone, (Group 1, No. 1), or legato groups contrasted with staccato ones, (Group 2, No. 4).

2 **Cadences.** The end of a phrase, from the harmonic standpoint, is marked by a *cadence.* Harmonic *cadences* are of two general types, the *full cadence* and the half or *semicadence.* Full cadences are of two kinds, *authentic,* V-I, and *plagal,* IV-I. When combined they form a *complete* full cadence, IV-V-I. Since the supertonic chord also supplies the two scale tones not included in the tonic and dominant harmonies, a complete cadence may also be formed with II-V-I.

The finality of a full cadence depends to a certain extent on the *position* of the final chord. If it is in the position of the 3rd or 5th we may call it an *open* full cadence; if the root appears in the soprano, it is a *closed* full cadence.

As the full cadence is the musical equivalent of the *period* which marks the end of a sentence, so the semicadence is the musical *comma,* indicating a partial close. Harmonically it is expressed by any pair of chords of which the second is the *dominant.* The commonest forms are I-V, IV-V, II-V, and VI-V.

In all cases where a melody appears to be symmetrically divided in half, the first phrase will probably end with either a semicadence, (Group 1, No. 3), or an *open* full cadence, (Group 1, No. 4).

3 **Procedure:**

(1) Determine the cadences, writing in both Roman numerals and the indicated bass notes.

(2) Observe that any given melody note may be harmonized with three different triads (except scale-steps 2, 4, and 7, which are limited to two triads apiece, the leading tone triad not being available.) It is important to consider *all* the possibilities, as some may be much better than others.

(3) If the melody moves stepwise, the chord must change.

(4) If the melody repeats a tone, it is usually best to change the chord, unless the first of two repeated tones ends a phrase, and the second begins a new one.

(5) If the melody skips, select a chord containing both notes and repeat it. If this is not possible, or results in a bad root progression, change the chord. In harmonizing a fourth-leap in the melody, if the same chord is not repeated the only possible change is in Class II, (roots down a third). A Class I progression produces bad consecutives, and a Class III progression results in a violation of the *rule of similar motion.*

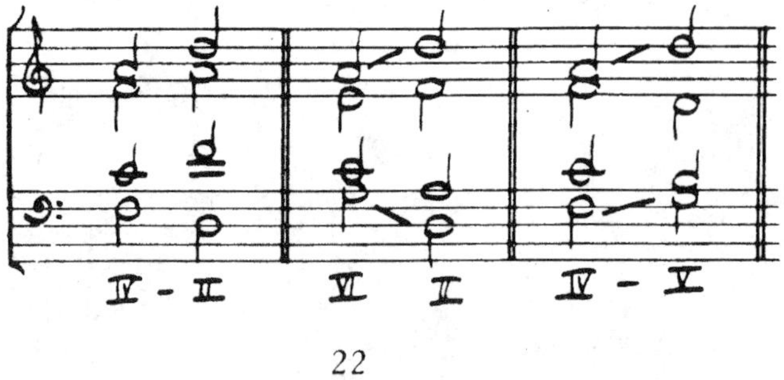

(6) The tendency of the supertonic into the dominant is nearly as strong as that of dominant into tonic; carefully avoid the progression II - I, therefore, unless specially indicated. Thus the melodic progression fa - re - me (4 - 2 - 3) or fa - re - do (4 - 2 - 1) in any key should always be harmonized with IV - V - I (VI) or with II - V - I. Note examples in Group 1, No. 1, and Group 2, No. 2.

(7) A change of chord produces an *harmonic accent;* a repeated chord does not; it is of importance that the harmonic accents be made to correspond with the natural rhythm of the melody, otherwise a disturbing effect of syncopation will result. This is particularly true in triple time, see Group 1, No. 2, third measure. The first two notes should be harmonized with the tonic chord, and the change to subdominant made on the third beat.

(8) The heaviest rhythmic accent is on the down beat of each measure; therefore the chord should always be changed over the bar-line, unless otherwise specified.

(9) Unless otherwise indicated, all exercises begin with the tonic chord, and end with an *authentic* cadence.

(10) *Always write the complete bass part first,* including the Roman numerals, before filling in the inner parts. Violations of the rules of *consecutives* and of *similar motion* are thus much more readily detected. In case of doubt, write the interval numbers made by the soprano and bass parts between the lines, and observe the results. Turn all stems for the soprano and tenor parts *up,* and for the bass and alto *down.*

MELODIES TO BE HARMONIZED

GROUP 1. Available Chords: I - IV - V

GROUP 2. Available Chords: I - II - IV - V

GROUP 3. Available Chords: I - II - IV - V - VI

GROUP 4. Available Chords: I - II - III - IV - V - VI

CHAPTER VIII

FIRST INVERSIONS OF TRIADS

1 When any other note than the root appears in the bass, a triad is said to be inverted. There are two possible inversions, the first having the third in the bass, and the second inversion the fifth. The pattern for the first inversion of a major triad is found in the *harmonic series,* partials 5, 6 and 8.

Note that the fundamental tone (C) of the series occurs as the *upper* tone of both intervals of which the chord is composed; the tones are in a sense *suspended downward* from the root, and in this position the chord is less stable than in its original form. It would be quite unsatisfactory as the final chord in an harmonic sentence; but the use of first inversions produces a smoother and more melodic bass, as well as improvements in the voice leading of the inner parts.

2 **Figuring.** In order to distinguish them from root triads, first inversions are indicated by the figure 6 placed to the right of the Roman numeral indicating the number-name of the root. A complete figuring presents a numerical picture of a chord, *counted from the bass note upwards.* A triad figures 1 - 3 - 5, a first inversion 1 - 3 - 6; hence the figure 6 is sufficient to indicate the first inversion, and such chords are often referred to as *sixth-chords,* (but be careful not to confuse them with the triad on VI).

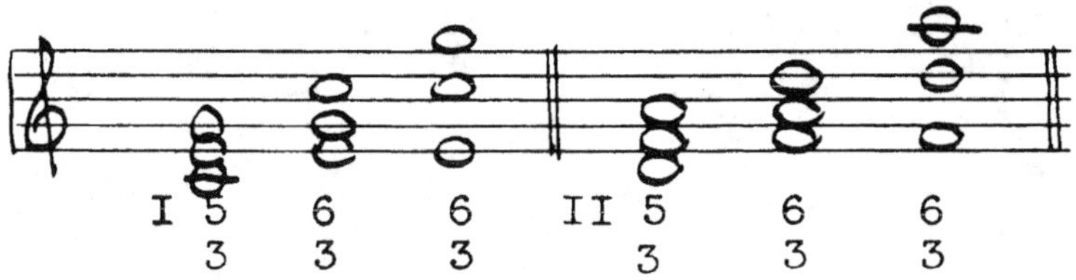

3 **Doubling.** Any tone of a first inversion may be doubled. The doubling of the *major third,* however, should be avoided unless it can be left *stepwise by contrary motion,* and in four part writing *the leading tone is almost never doubled.* The tonality of an harmonic phrase is emphasized by the doubling of its *primary tones,* the first, fourth and fifth scale-steps. Since these tones are the thirds of VI, II and III respectively, it follows that *the secondary triads frequently double their thirds.*

The primary triads will normally double either root or fifth; from the standpoint of voice leading, the best tone to double in a first inversion is the nearest one to those that precede and follow in the same part.

4 **Root Progressions.** The use of first inversions does not in any way alter the general procedure with regard to the three classes of chord-root progression. Particular care must be used to observe the rules of consecutives and of similar motion. With regard to the rule of contrary motion in Class III, if one of the chords is inverted the usual result will be two parts moving in contrary motion to the other two parts.

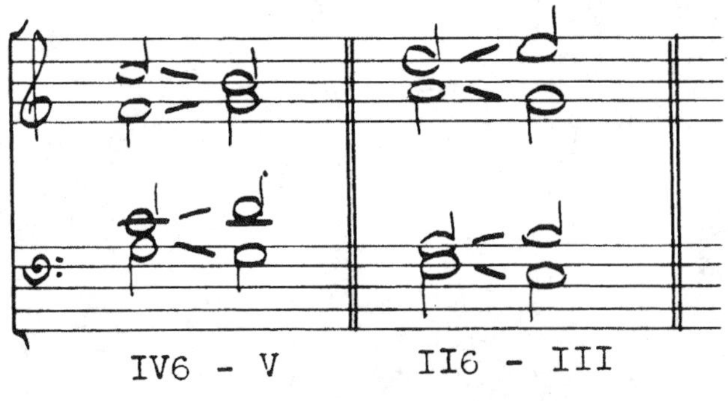

5 **The consonant fourth.** The perfect fourth, whose upper tone is its fundamental, was regarded by early composers as a dissonance when its lower tone appeared in the bass. In the first inversion of a triad, this interval is enclosed by the wider interval of a sixth, gaining thereby in consonant value. For purposes of analysis it is convenient to recognize this difference by referring to a fourth whose lower tone is in the bass or lowest part as a *dissonant* fourth, and one which occurs between upper parts as a *consonant* fourth. (This type of "dissonant" perfect fourth, however, must be carefully distinguished from the *tritone,* which is a far stronger and more active dissonance.)

Consonant fourths may be used in parallel motion; therefore *consecutive fourths may be used between any of the upper voices.*

6 The following illustrations show some of the possibilities. In Ex. 1 the first inversions follow root positions of the same chords. In Ex. 2 first inversions alternate with other chords in root position. Ex. 3 includes the VI_6 and the III_6 which are best in Class I progressions.

Ex. 1

Ex. 2

Ex. 3

The most frequently used of all first inversions is the II_6 as a substitute for IV in the *complete cadence.* It has the advantage of harmonizing the melodically important supertonic note, while retaining the tonally strong fourth scale step in the bass, a tone which is often emphasized by doubling, Ex. 4-b.

Ex. 4-a. b.

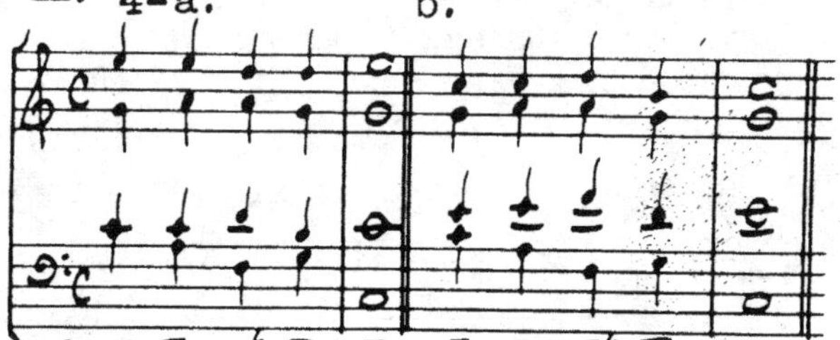

7 **The leading tone sixth.** The *tritone,* either as augmented fourth or diminished fifth, may occur between the *upper* tones of a first inversion chord whose bass note is the second scale-step. This chord may be referred to as *leading tone sixth,* and indicated by L 6. The active dissonance of the tritone is *resolved* by moving the leading tone to the key tone, and the other voice *stepwise down.* Thus the augmented fourth resolves by *stepwise expansion,* and the diminished fifth by *stepwise contraction,* Ex. 5-a and b. However, in certain cases, in order to avoid a bad doubling or an incomplete chord of resolution, the tritone is resolved in parallel motion to a perfect fourth, Ex. 5-c. The effect of the leading tone is strongly dominant, and the dominant tone is in fact the fundamental of this dissonant chord; hence its normal resolution is always to the tonic, though a resolution to the submediant is also possible, Ex. 5-d.

8 **Consecutive first inversions.** Since the roots are in the upper parts of all first inversion chords, their use in succession produces a topheavy and rather weak effect, and such progressions should be used sparingly. If the soprano and bass move scalewise in parallel sixths, a series of first inversions in Class III may occur. The *doubling tone must move in contrary motion* to the others; if it moved in similar motion it would produce both parallel fifths and octaves. The odd doublings and skips involved limit the usefulness of this device, Ex. 6.

9 **Harmonization of melodies.** The *leading tone sixth* chord provides us with an additional *authentic full cadence,* in which the supertonic note occurs in the bass. It also supplies an additional chord to harmonize the 2nd, 4th and 7th scale-steps. Fourth-leaps in the melody may be treated with first inversions of the same chord or an alternate, (Class II) but avoid the hidden fifths in Ex. 9, (Class III).

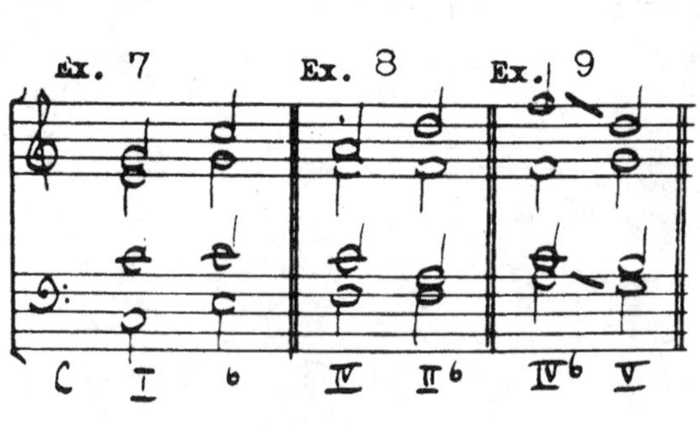

MELODIES, GROUP I. AVAILABLE CHORDS: I - IV - V

1.

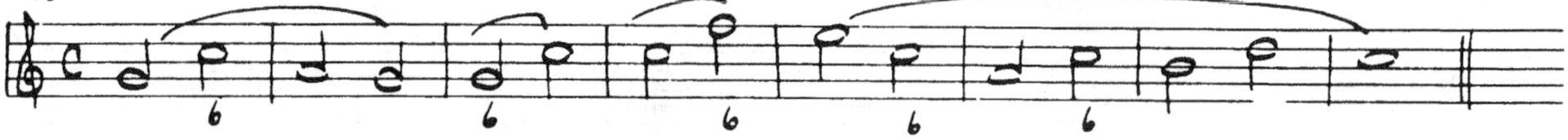

2.

3.

4.

5.

GROUP II. AVAILABLE CHORDS: I - II - III - IV - V - VI

1.

2.

3.

4.

5.

GROUP III, with L6, indicated by *

CHAPTER IX

SECOND INVERSIONS OF TRIADS

1 The second inversion of a triad exposes the lower note of the "dissonant" fourth in the bass or lowest part. This is the weakest position of the triad, and throughout the classical period was considered an active combination requiring resolution to the triad *having the same bass tone as root.* The upper tone of the fourth was considered the "dissonating" and therefore active tone, which resolved stepwise downward taking the sixth with it in parallel motion. The reasons for this are not at all clear, as the upper tone of the fourth is its fundamental, and theoretically the interval could be resolved in many other ways. It is probably a survival of the leading tone suspension which was a feature of almost every cadence in the fifteenth and sixteenth centuries.

2 **Figuring.** Second inversions present the numerical picture $^6_4$ counted upwards from the bass, and are usually referred to as *six-four chords.*

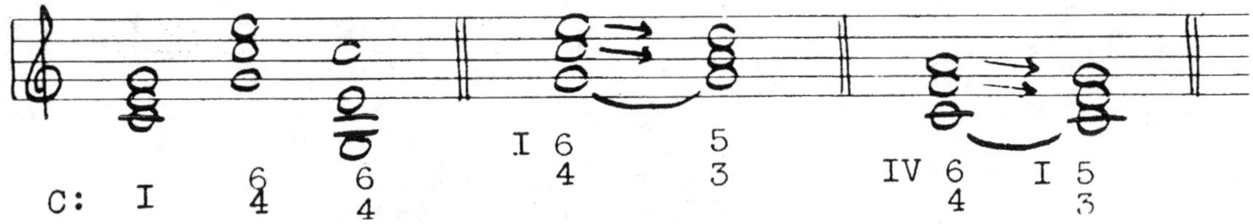

3 **Doubling.** With very rare exceptions, the *fifth* (bass tone) is doubled.

4 **Uses.** In classical practice the I$^6_4$ and the IV$^6_4$ are the only second inversions used with any frequency; according to the formula given above it would be impossible for the second inversion of III, with leading tone in the bass, to resolve at all, and as a six-four of the leading tone triad would expose the tritone in the bass, this inversion is also unavailable.

The formula I$^6_4$ - V is a very common form of *semicadence;* the tonic six-four chord almost invariably displaces the dominant *on the strong beat,* and may therefore be referred to as a *deferred dominant;* the doubled tones remain the same, and the fourth and sixth *"resolve"* stepwise down to the third and fifth of the V. It is also a common factor in all kinds of *complete cadences,* and usually occupies a strong rhythmic position in the measure, though it sometimes occurs as the second chord in a triple measure.

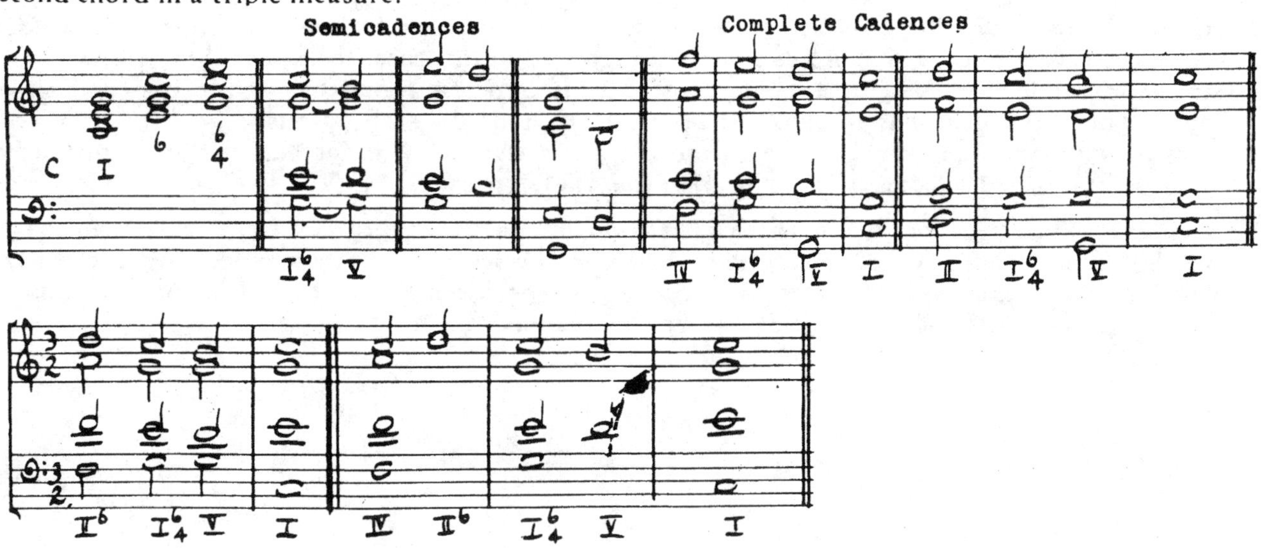

5 **The returning six-four chord.** Between a fundamental triad and its exact repetition a second inversion having the same bass tone is sometimes inserted. The root and third of the six-four chord are in effect *neighbor tones* of the third and fifth of the triad which they have just left and to which they immediately return; the chord may therefore be called a *returning six-four chord;* its root is a fifth below that of the chord to which it returns. Ex. 1.

6 **The passing six-four chord.** A second inversion is sometimes inserted between a fundamental position of a chord and its own first inversion, or vice versa. The second inversion is that of the chord whose root lies a fourth below that of the first chord. The common tone is kept in the same voice. Because of the fact that two of the remaining tones pass scalewise from one tone of the first chord to another of the same chord when it recurs, a six-four used in this way may be termed a *passing six-four chord,* Ex. 2.

Ex. 1

Ex. 2

7 **The suspending six-four chord.** A second inversion may appear on the down beat or other accented portion of a bar, when directly preceded by its own fundamental position. It then resolves to the triad whose root lies a fourth below, following the pattern of the semicadence. Since the fourth and sixth of the six-four chord appear to hold back or "suspend" the normal progression of the parts involved from one triad to another, it may be called a *suspending six-four chord,* Ex. 3.

Ex. 3

8 **In chord repetitions** the bass may leap from root to third or fifth of the chord in any desired sequence; the rules of doubling are sometimes ignored in this case, the upper three parts remaining stationary while the bass leaps about. This effect is common in marches and in dance music of all kinds, where the principal emphasis is upon the rhythm. In such patterns the fifth of the chord hardly ever occurs on an accent; from the harmonic standpoint no actual six-four chord is heard, as the root or third remains the true bass for the whole group.

9 **Sequences.** A repetition of a musical pattern upon some other degree of the scale than that upon which it first occurs is called a *sequence.* An harmonic sequence, in its simplest form, consists of a pattern of two chords. These may be triads in root position. Ex. 1, a triad in root position and a first inversion, Ex. 2 and 3, or consecutive first inversions, Ex. 4.

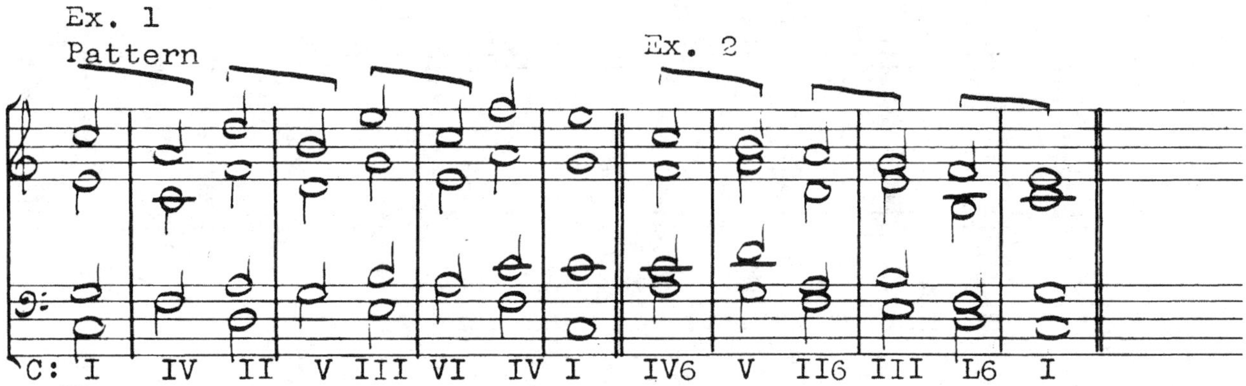

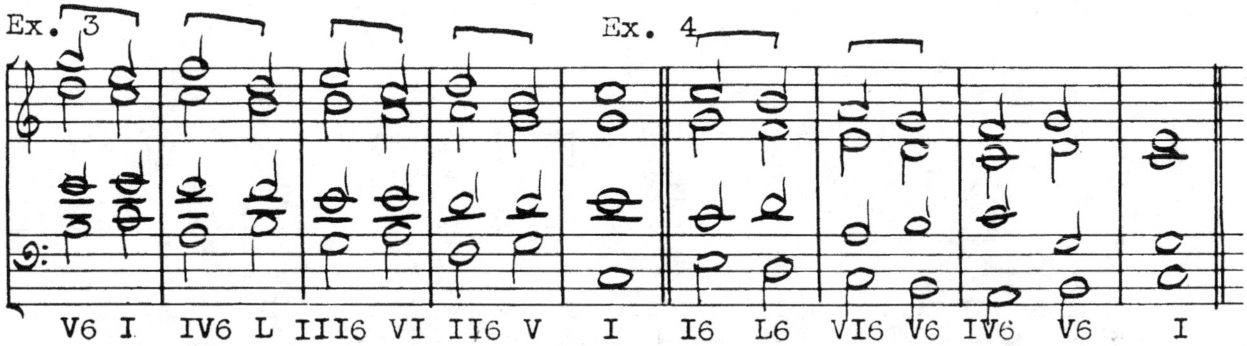

The suspending six-four chord also lends itself readily to sequential treatment, Ex. 5.

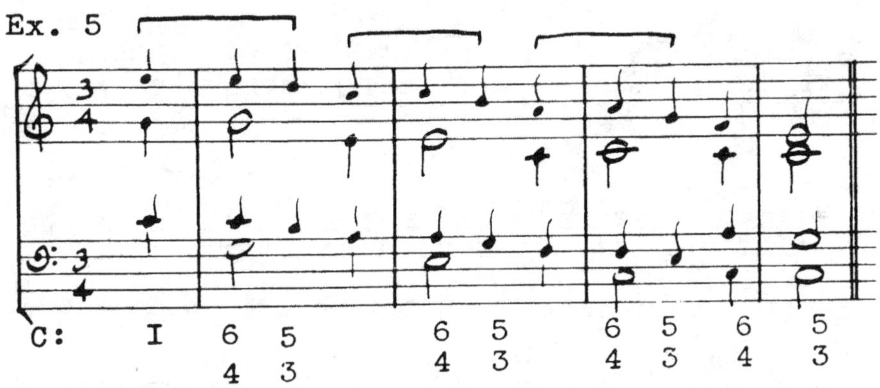

Note: In order not to break the sequence pattern in passages of this type it is permissible to double the leading tone, and to make occasional use of the leading tone triad uninverted, Ex. 3, meas. 2, and 4 meas. 2.

MELODIES. GROUP I. Cadences with Tonic $^6_4$ indicated by *

Group II. Passing and returning second inversions.

Group III. Sequences; suspending second inversions.

5.

6.

7.

Keyboard Exercises. 1. Play the Group 1 cadences in all keys. Do not leave one key for the next until some facility has been gained through several repetitions of the pattern.

2. Play complete phrases in ¾ time using the indicated beginnings and selecting a suitable cadence from those given. When this can be done at MM. 60 without hesitation or error, transpose up by whole steps: C - D - E - F sharp - A flat - B flat; then down from B by whole steps: B - A - G - F - E flat - D flat.

3. Repeat the same process with the cadences which include tonic six-four, Group 2. As these cadences are three measures in length, only one measure beginning is necessary to make four measure phrases.

4. Improvise periods of two phrases in similar style. The first phrase should end with a semicadence in measure four.

5. Harmonize the ascending and descending major scale as indicated. Transpose to all keys.

Group 1. Cadences

1. 2. 3. 4.

5.

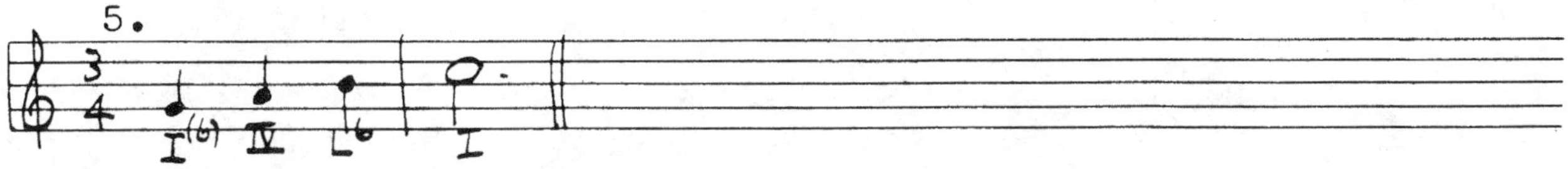

Beginnings of phrases

1. with cadence 1 or 4

2. with any cadence

3. with cadence 4

4. with cadence 2, 3, 4

Group 2. Cadences with I^6_4

Beginnings:

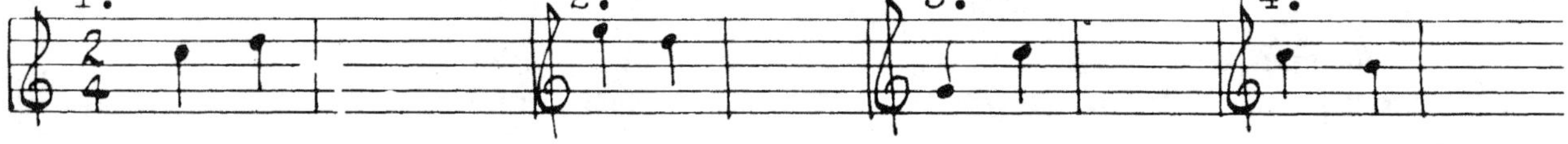

Scales.

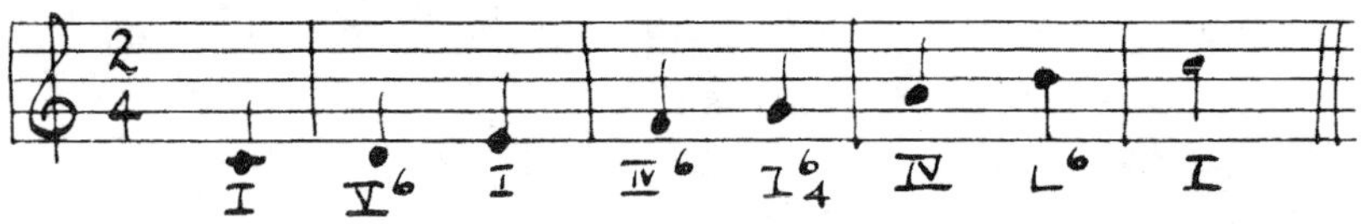

CHAPTER X

THE MINOR MODE

1 **The relative minor scale.** Reference was made in Chapter I to the fact that each major scale has a relative minor scale beginning and ending on its sixth degree. In minor keys, therefore, the signature is the same as that of the major key whose tonic is the third degree of the minor scale. The semitones lie between the second and third, and the fifth and sixth scale-steps; as a result the thirds of both tonic and subdominant chords are minor, resulting in the characteristic "dark" color of the minor mode.

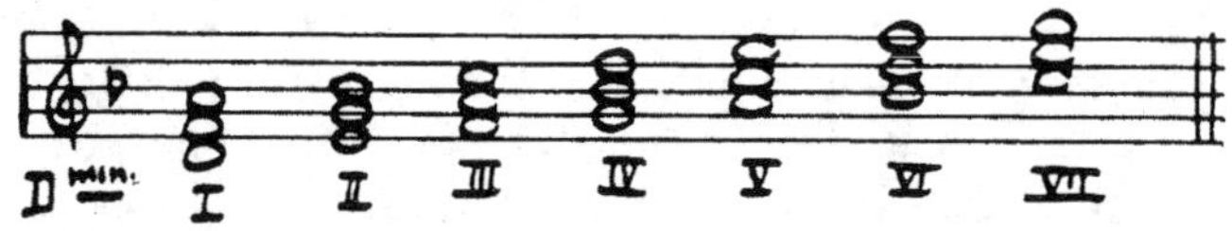

2 **The harmonic minor scale.** Observing the triads erected upon the various degrees of the natural minor scale, we see that they are merely a rearrangement of the triads of the relative major key. The tonic, the subdominant and the dominant are minor, the mediant, submediant and subtonic are major, and the supertonic diminished. The lack of a leading tone is, however, a fatal defect from the *tonal* standpoint, which must be remedied, in all cases where clear tonal definition is necessary, by raising the seventh scale step a semitone with the proper accidental, resulting in what is known as the *harmonic minor scale.*

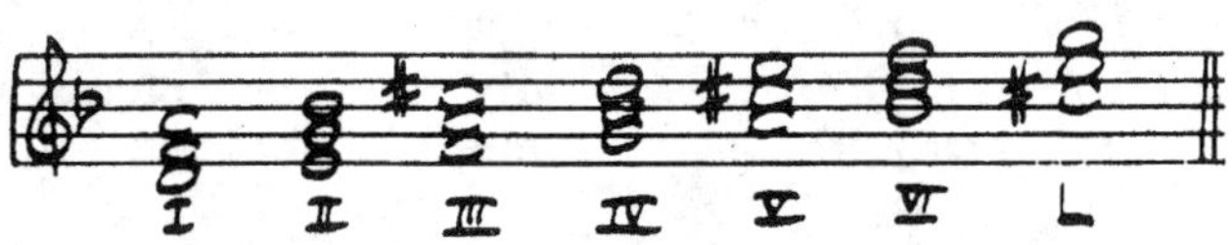

This produces a major dominant triad and a diminished leading tone triad, exactly like those of the *parallel* major key (i. e. beginning on the same tone) and an augmented mediant triad whose usefulness is somewhat limited. In order to distinguish clearly the two chords on the two different seventh degrees of the minor scale, we will call the unaltered seventh scale-step (a whole tone below the tonic) the *subtonic,* and indicate it, as well as the triad upon it with the figure VII, while the diminished triad on the chromatically raised seventh scale-step will be designated *leading tone* as in major keys. A leading tone triad is therefore *always diminished* and available normally only in its first inversion. A subtonic triad, being major, has the same availability as other major triads.

3 **The melodic minor scale.** In the harmonic minor scale the interval between the sixth and seventh scale-steps is an augmented second. On keyboard instruments this interval is the same as a minor third, but is actually felt to be considerably larger, and was carefully avoided by the classical composers except for an occasional broken chord arrangement over dominant harmony. A possible explanation for this lies in the strong polarity or tonal attraction of the tonic and dominant. Thus the minor submediant, only a semitone above the dominant, tends to fall back upon it, while the leading tone has an even stronger tendency up into the tonic. Thus a gulf is created betwen the two tones which is seldom crossed. Therefore avoid *the augmented second as a melodic interval.*

In order to pass from the sixth to the seventh scale-steps in the same part it is necessary to use the so-called *melodic form* of the minor scale, wherein the sixth scale-step as well as the seventh is chromatically raised. As a result the upper tetrachord (scale of four tones) is indistinguishable from the same portion of the parallel major scale. Harmonically, the raised sixth scale-step produces a minor triad on the second degree, a major triad on the fourth, and a diminished triad on the sixth.

The descending form of the *melodic minor scale* is identical with its natural form, the sixth and seventh tones being left unaltered.

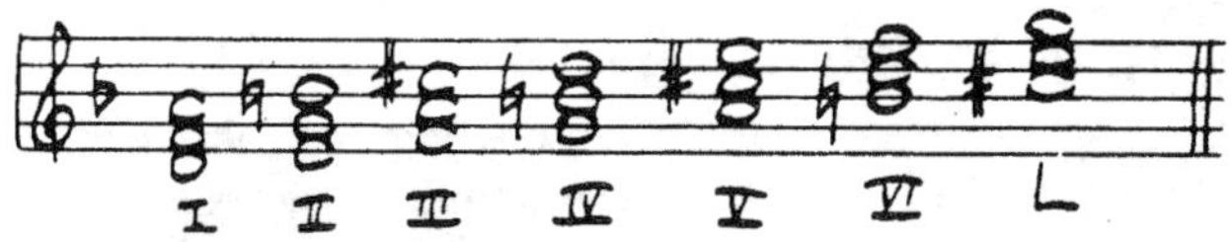

The various forms of the minor scale produce two diminished triads in addition to the one on the leading tone. They all suffer from the same deficiency: as they contain no perfect fifth, they are without root. The result is that they appear only as first inversions. The augmented triad on III is a chord of very limited usefulness. The augmented fifth is actually sharper than the enharmonic minor sixth, but still hardly a dissonance. There is some conflict of upper partials of the two major thirds, each of which strives to establish its lower tone as the *root*. The potency of the leading tone is so great in this respect that if the chord is placed in its first inversion it will almost certainly be heard as a dominant chord. The tonal ambiguity of any chord consisting of *equal intervals* should be apparent.

4 **Treatment of seventh scale-tone.** From the harmonic standpoint, the color of the minor mode derives largely from its minor third and minor sixth scale steps, especially as they affect the tonic and subdominant triads. From the melodic standpoint, it should be noted that when the seventh scale-tone rises stepwise it should be a leading tone, and if it is approached stepwise from below in the same voice the sixth scale-step must also be raised. The raised sixth tone and natural seventh produce an immediate ambiguity of tonal center which should be carefully avoided. It should be obvious that if the leading tone is not heard at frequent intervals a passage in the minor mode will tend to revert to the relative major. Observe carefully what the seventh scale-tone does, in whatever voice it appears. If it moves *stepwise upward,* it should be chromatically raised, Ex. 1 and 2.

If it moves *stepwise downward,* it remains unaltered, Ex. 3 and 4.

Chromatic alterations of a repetition of the same note in any voice are forbidden in strict writing, Ex. 5, tenor voice. Furthermore, the altered and unaltered forms of the same note may not appear in different voices of two successive chords. The result is a *cross relation,* Ex. 6.

If the melodic succession 8 - 7 - 6 is used in any voice, the sixth and seventh steps remain unaltered, Ex. 4. If the melodic succession 6 - 7 - 8 is used in any voice, the sixth and seventh steps are both raised a semitone, Ex. 7. Examples 8 and 9 further illustrate this in the bass part. Examples 10 and 11 are harmonized versions of the descending and ascending forms of the melodic minor scale. Observe in Examples 7, 11 and 12 three different ways of harmonizing the melodic succession 6 - 7 - 8.

Recall that diminished triads are available only in their *first inversions.* This applies not only to the leading tone triad in cadences, but to the unaltered supertonic and the altered submediant triads, Ex. 12.

The augmented mediant triad in root position is of very limited usefulness, the only good progression being into the submediant, Ex. 13.

MELODIES. GROUP I. Uninverted Triads.

1. **Available chords: I - IV - V**

2.

3.

4.

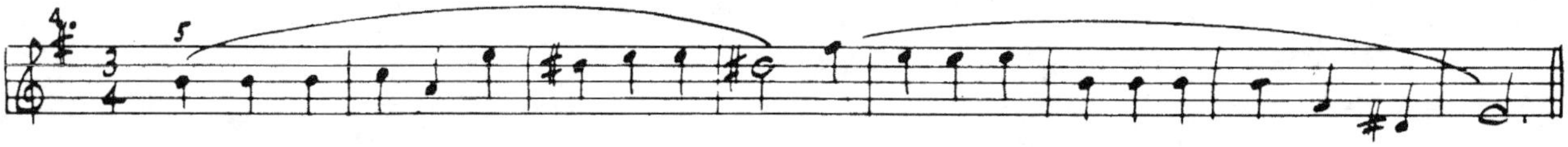

5.

Available chords: I - II - III - IV - V - VI

6.

7.

8.

GROUP II. With Inversions.
Available chords: I to VII inclusive.

CHAPTER XI

HARMONIZATION OF FIGURED BASSES

1 **Interpretation of figuring.** In harmonizing a given bass part, it is necessary to give particular attention to the melodic qualities of the upper parts, especially the soprano. If the bass is figured, there is no choice of chords, — they are all predetermined. Bass notes not provided with figures are the *roots of triads;* the figure $_6$ indicates that the given bass note is the third of a triad in its first inversion, and $^6_4$ indicates the second inversion, with the fifth in the bass. A single bass note may have two chords written above it, each occupying a part of its time value. This is particularly true of the six-four chord, resolving to a five-three on the same bass note. In that case it is usual to indicate the change of chord by the figure $_5$ or $^5_3$; the rhythmic arrangement will follow the natural patterns indicated by the time signature and general treatment.

2 **Accidentals.** In the minor mode, accidentals will occur in the figuring. A sharp, flat or cancel below a bass note, without other figures, indicates that the *third above* the given bass note is modified as indicated. Other chromatically altered tones are indicated by number as well as accidental. At present these altered tones will always be the sixth or seventh scale-steps of the minor scale in question.

3 **Two solutions.** In all work from a figured bass the student is strongly urged to make at least *two* solutions, and then combine the best points of both, as it is very unlikely that he will succeed in finding the best arrangement of the parts at the first trial. Remembering that *a bass figuring is a numerical picture of a chord, counted from the bass note upwards,* the first step is to fill in the Roman numerals, indicating chord-roots. The second step is to fill in the indicated tones above the bass part. The third step is to examine the results carefully for the best melodic groups, which should then be transferred to a new score, in which the bass and soprano are *completely worked out* before filling in the inner parts. The fourth and final step is to *check each part with all the parts above it* for consecutives and other melodic and contrapuntal defects.

The example below has been worked twice, the first solution illustrating some common errors and the second how these may be corrected. The following points should be especially noted:

a) Avoid placing the common tone in the soprano, with consequent melodic dullness, Ex. 1, meas. 2.

b) All leaps wider than a third should be made, as far as possible, on a *chord repetition,* with or without inversion, Ex. 2, meas. 2 and 3, and not with a change of root, particularly in Class I, Ex. 1, meas. 2 and 3.

c) Avoid separating notes having a natural melodic cohesion, such as the keytone and leading tone in Ex. 1, meas. 2, which belong in the same part, Ex. 2.

d) Two skips in the same direction should outline a chord, not a discord combination, Ex. 1, meas. 3.

Ex. 1

Ex. 2

Note: Figures above the staff refer to the chord tone to be used in the soprano, counted from the bass note upwards. In case of doubt, a plus sign (+) indicates the higher, and a minus sign (—) the lower of two possible notes within the soprano range.

FIGURED BASSES

1.

2.

3.

4.

5.

6.

7.

8.

GROUP II. WITH SIX-FOUR

GROUP III. MINOR MODE

CHAPTER XII

FUNDAMENTAL HARMONIC RELATIONS

The material of the preceding chapters may now be reviewed and summarized, in order to emphasize the general principles underlying all normal harmonic writing. We shall consider in turn the factors of chord-root progression, harmonic counterpoint, doubling, and harmonic rhythm.

I Chord-Root Progression

1 **Tonality.** Clear *tonal definition* is best achieved through emphasis on the primary triads, I - IV - V. The leading tone sixth is also dominant in effect, and therefore a strong tonal determinant. The supertonic triad, and especially the supertonic sixth, with the *primary* fourth scale-step in the bass, replaces the subdominant in many complete cadences. The other secondary triads, III and VI, are much less frequently used; they provide variety, as alternates for primary chords, and a certain amount of harmonic color.

2 **Syntax.** The normal *syntax* of chord-root progressions is easily established by observing the practice of the great composers. In the following sentences: "Table on the lies book the", and "The book lies on the table" we have examples of bad and good *syntax* in English grammar. While chords in themselves do not possess the same clear cut and sharply defined meanings as words, never-the-less a definite normal order can be determined, both on the basis of the physical properties of the chords themselves and through the associations acquired by these progressions in standard practice.

We have seen that normal progressive order between two chords results when the root of the second chord is a *new tone,* not contained in the first chord. From this standpoint, progressive order may be stated as follows:

Progressive ⟶
I - VI - IV - II - (L6) - V - III - I
⟵ Regressive

However, in Class III progressions, the roots are always new tones; Here the progressive and regressive order seems to be determined by the relative value of the chords as *tonal determinants,* that is, their closeness or remoteness from the key center, which gives us the following order in Class III:

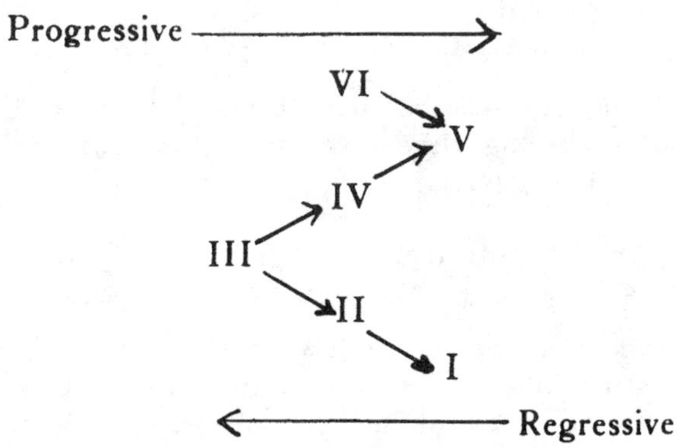

The regressive order I - V is as common as any of the progressive root movements. The *plagal cadence,* IV - I, in which the root of the second chord is contained in the first, appears to be an exception to the above classification. However it should be noted that in themselves the progressions I - V and IV - I are indistinguishable from each other; their place in any tonal scheme is dependent upon *other tonal determinants.*

Regressive movements are not by any means to be considered bad or objectionable. Some are quite common, and others properly used add color and interest to the harmonic texture. In standard practice the great majority of chord-root movements are, however, progressive.'

II Harmonic Counterpoint

1 **Contrapuntal Units.** The term counterpoint is usually applied to the art of combining melodies, with emphasis on the voice leading. In harmonic counterpoint we are only concerned at present with the simplest kind of chord connection. A *melodic unit* consists of two successive tones; an *harmonic unit* consists of two tones sounded together, (an interval); a *contrapuntal unit* consists of four tones, which are a combination of two melodic and two harmonic units. In the progression of two chords in four parts there are six contrapuntal units, as follows: bass and tenor, bass and alto, bass and soprano, tenor and alto, tenor and soprano, alto and soprano.

2 **The Primary Diaphony.** An analysis of any type of music, whether its interest be mainly harmonic or mainly contrapuntal, will quickly reveal the fundamental importance of the bass or lowest part in its harmonic construction. Associated with it will be a second part, usually the highest, which will have almost equal importance in determining or outlining the harmonic succession, and these two parts provide a basic outline of the chord structure, to which the other parts, no matter how numerous, merely add details, confirming, elaborating or embellishing the original sketch.

To these two basic and fundamental parts we may apply the term *primary diaphony* in order to indicate their ruling or governing importance in the harmonic scheme. The lower of the two parts will always be the bass or lowest sounding part. In some types of contrapuntal music the part next in importance will be a middle voice, with the upper part or parts providing contrapuntal decoration or embellishment, but in almost all other cases the Primary Diaphony will consist of the top and bottom, or "outside" voices, (soprano and bass).

The *primary diaphony* should not be thought of as an exercise in two part counterpoint, however similar it may seem. In many elaborate scores the bass part frequently consists of no more than the occasional sounding of a few harmonic fundamentals. Nevertheless, even in music where the interest is wholly harmonic, the *diaphony* will to some extent be governed by contrapuntal considerations. These contrapuntal procedures, as they apply to two-part writing, were thoroughly and completely worked out in the sixteenth century, and we shall summarize them here, noting a few changes and relaxations possible when considering two parts as an harmonic outline:

1) *Harmonic intervals* which may be used are limited to the following consonances:

Perfect unison and octave
Perfect fifth
Major and minor third
Major and minor sixth

2) *Melodic intervals* which may be used include all major, minor and perfect intervals up to and including the octave, but excluding the major sixth and both minor and major sevenths, as well as all augmented and diminished intervals.

3) *Kinds of Motion;* in the simultaneous progression of two voices from one interval to another four kinds of motion are possible: parallel, similar, oblique and contrary.

Parallel Motion results whenever intervals of the same number-name follow each other, whether their quality is the same or not. Thus a major third followed by a minor third is considered as parallel. Because of their lack of independence parallel unisons, octaves and fifths are forbidden. Therefore the only available parallel motion is in thirds and sixths; more than three in succession are usually dull, and care must be taken not to produce the false relation of the tritone by sounding two *major* thirds in succession, moving by whole steps.

Similar Motion is produced when both parts move in the same direction, but different distances. This is good if the second interval is a third or a sixth; in harmonic writing similar approach to a fifth or an octave is possible if the *upper part moves stepwise.*

Oblique Motion occurs when only one part moves, the other part retaining the same tone.

Contrary Motion is always preferable to any other kind, as better serving the interests of individuality and independence of the voices. All combinations of consonant intervals are good in contrary motion, with two exceptions: (1) octaves and fifths by contrary motion are considered the same as by parallel motion; (2) thirds, either major or minor, followed by fifths produce a dull or harsh effect which somewhat limits their usefulness. If the third be major, a tritone is produced. The reverse procedure, fifth followed by major third, seems less objectionable, probably because it is associated with the harmonic formula IV - V, in which it invariably occurs.

4) *Additional Possibilities.*

a) The "dissonant" fourth may be used to imply a six-four chord; in the cadence it will *always* consist of the keynote above the fifth scale-tone, and will be directly followed by the third having the same bass tone.

b) The melodic interval of the tritone as a *downward* diminished fifth may be written in the upper part when implying the progression II - V.

c) The melodic interval of the major sixth may be used in the upper part when proceeding from a triad to its own first inversion, and vice versa.

d) The melodic interval of the sixth (major or minor) may be used in the bass, if it proceeds *downward* from the root to the *third of the same chord.*

The following table of *contrapuntal units* illustrates most of the above points.

CONTRAPUNTAL UNITS

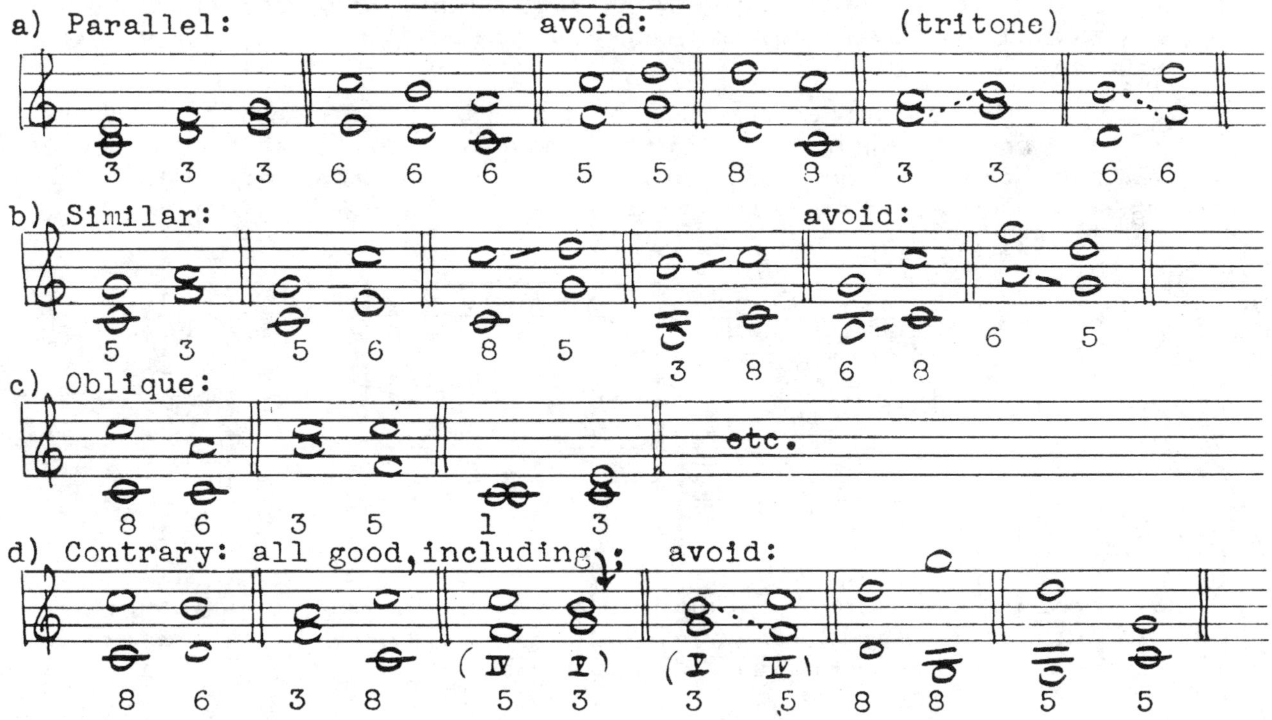

3 Cadences. The bass part of a diaphony will often have much less melodic cohesion than a contrapuntal bass. We have seen that the simplest of all chord progressions are those in Class I, where a bass part sounding roots only would proceed by leaps of a fourth and fifth. Some inversions may of course be used, but as they are far less stable than root positions the demands of tonal definition will normally require a majority of roots in the bass.

This is especially true at the conclusions of phrases, where the tonality is most sharply defined. Complete tonal definition is only achieved through the sounding of all the notes of the scale, and a *complete* cadence, therefore, will consist of the formula IV - V - I, or its alternate II - V - I. The progression IV - V - I has the advantage of using in progressive order the two chords most closely related to the tonic. The II, however, contains the melodically useful second scale tone, and replaces the IV in a great many cadences. So strong is the cadence feeling for the *subdominant root,* however, that the supertonic chord when used at this point is nearly always in its *first inversion,* thus preserving the pattern of scale steps 4-5-1 as the *primary cadence bass.*

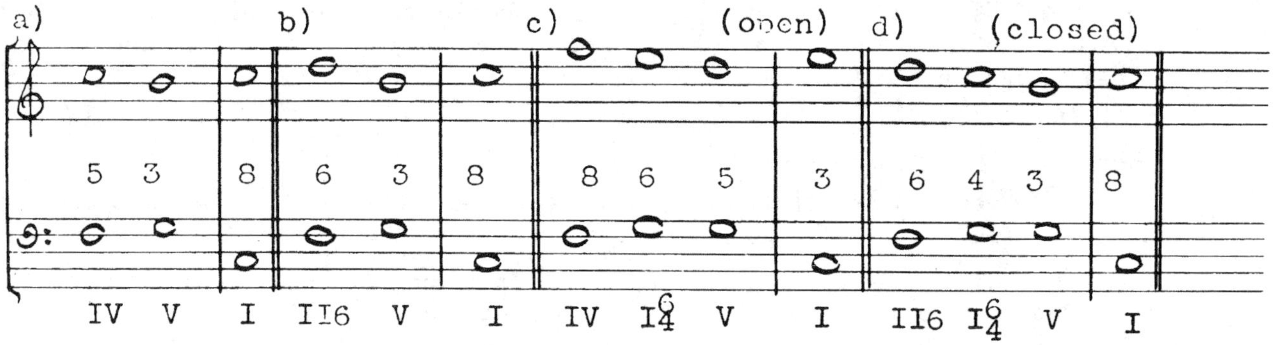

Stepwise melodic movement in the cadence melody frequently requires the use of a tone of the tonic chord between the IV or II and the V. In this case the second inversion of the tonic is invariably used, thus avoiding a redundant double full cadence (IV - I - V - I) and preserving the *primary cadence bass.*

One further type of complete cadence should be mentioned here. It replaces the dominant chord with the leading tone sixth, which, as will be demonstrated later, actually has the dominant root as its fundamental tone, though in this case it is implied rather than sounded. The resulting bass pattern is *tonally weaker,* but *melodically stronger* than the primary cadence bass.

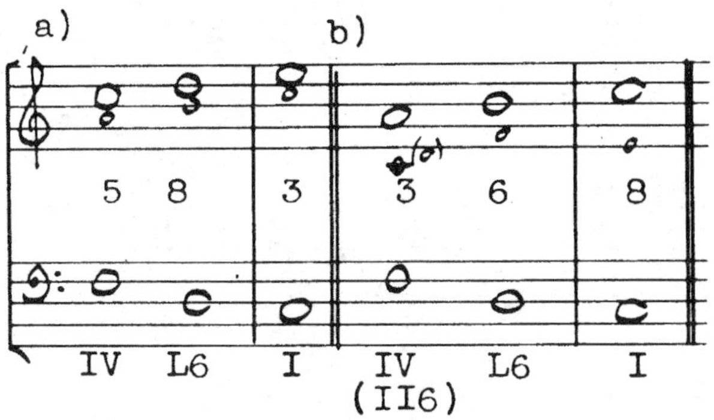

The *semicadence* is produced by placing the dominant chord in root position at the end of a phrase; it is often preceded by I $^6_4$ but any suitable progression leading to V may be used. As the dominant root is essential in the bass, the L_6 is not available.

4 **Inner voices.** The rules of two part counterpoint are also applied to the progression of any of the inner voices, or an inner voice with an outer voice, with only two important exceptions:

1) parallel fourths are permitted between any of the *upper* voices.

2) similar motion to an octave or a fifth is often unavoidable, and may be used when necessary.

III DOUBLING

It is now possible to make a complete statement of the rules which govern the selection of doubling tones in a texture consisting exclusively of triads. There are three of them; the *tonal rule,* the *harmonic rule,* and the *melodic rule.* Good doubling will be achieved only if all three rules are considered. In some cases the same doubling will satisfy all three rules; in many cases two rules will indicate the same doubling. In case of a definite conflict, a good decision will depend upon the student's artistic judgment, expressed in his ability to hear the relative strength of tones in a chord, and to appreciate the cohesion and force of tones in melodic and tonal relationships.

THE RULES OF DOUBLING

A. The Tonal Rule

A tonality is best defined and emphasized by doubling the first, fourth and fifth scale tones.

B. The Harmonic Rule

a) *Root doubling.* This is the strongest harmonic doubling for triads in root position. (The leading tone is *not* a root). Since the tonal and harmonic rules coincide for the primary triads, they nearly always double their roots.

The root doubling is good in first inversions, but practically *never* occurs in second inversions.

b) *Fifth doubling.* In root position this is rare, and requires melodic justification. In first inversions the fifth doubling is good, and the fifth is always doubled in second inversions.

c) *Third doubling.* The *minor* third is frequently doubled in secondary triads, either in root position or first inversion, in accordance with the tonal rule. The doubling of minor thirds in primary triads is less frequent.

Doubled *major* thirds are weak from the harmonic standpoint, and *always* require melodic justification.

C. The Melodic Rule

a) A doubled tone which can be reached and left *stepwise* is the best melodic doubling. A doubled tone which repeats or holds over the same tone is preferable to one that skips.

b) A *major* third may be doubled

1) to resolve the leading tone, as in the progression V - VI in minor keys, where the tonal rule also supports this doubling.

2) when it can be left *stepwise by contrary motion.*

3) to avoid bad consecutives.

IV HARMONIC RHYTHM

1 **Rhythmic Units.** The rhythmic position in a measure is often the determining factor in the choice of chords. The simplest rhythmic units are duple and triple. In a duple group or measure there is one strong and one weak beat. In a triple measure the usual feeling is strong-weak-weak, but the third beat may be felt as stronger than the second, though not so strong as the first.

2 **Harmonic Accent.** It is obvious that a change of chord produces an *harmonic accent.* The strength of the harmonic accent varies with the number of new tones introduced. Thus a change in Class III, (stepwise roots) is the strongest possible change, where only triads are concerned; a Class I change with two different tones and one common tone is less strong, and Class II changes, in which two tones remain the same, are the least strong. For practical purposes we may draw an arbitrary line at the half-way point, and say that if more than half of the tones are changed the effect is strong, otherwise it is weak. Thus changes in both Class I and Class III are strong, and weak changes include not only Class II but also rearrangements of the same chord, — inversions, and changes of position which retain the same bass tone.

3 **Syncopation.** It is normal for strong harmonic changes to coincide with strong beats, otherwise *syncopations* will appear. A syncopation will be produced in duple measure if a weak change is made from a weak beat to a succeeding strong beat, and in triple measure not only is the same thing true, but a particularly heavy syncopation results if a strong change is made from the first to the second beats and then a weak change from the second to the third. Of course if all the changes are strong no syncopation will result.

Exercises. In the following *unfigured basses* work out the *diaphony* first. Indicate complete figuring, including alternative roots where these are possible. The rhythm of the soprano will not necessarily coincide exactly with that of the given bass, but do not use any non-chord tones. (Above a given half-note the stepwise melody 5 - 6 or 6 - 5 may be written in quarters.) The diaphonies should be approved by the instructor before the inner parts are completed, and carefully checked from the standpoint of each of the four factors discussed in this chapter.

UNIFIGURED BASSES

4.

5.

6.

CHAPTER XIII

THE DOMINANT SEVENTH CHORD

1 The addition of the seventh above the root to any of the triads produces what is known as a seventh chord. The *dominant seventh chord,* which is the most frequently used of all seventh chords, consists of a minor seventh added to a major triad. Two dissonances, the seventh and the tritone are thus created, both of which require *resolution,* which, as already explained, involves the progression of a dissonant interval to one having a higher harmonic value (simpler ratio). Of the two tones of a dissonant interval, one is usually more active than the other; in the case of the minor seventh this is the seventh, which must invariably move to produce a real feeling of resolution. Leaving it by a leap breaks all feeling of continuity and is quite unsatisfactory, Ex. 1-b. The upward stepwise resolution causes it to become lost in the overtones of the root, thus seeming to disappear without resolving, (c). Resolutions in which it remains fixed while the lower tone moves are equally weak, (d, e). Thus the only good resolutions are those in which the seventh moves *stepwise downward,* forming the upper tone of a sixth, fifth or third. The sixth implies either I or III, but the latter is too much like V to be a strong resolution chord. The fifth implies VI, the third I or VI; therefore the best resolution chords are I and VI.

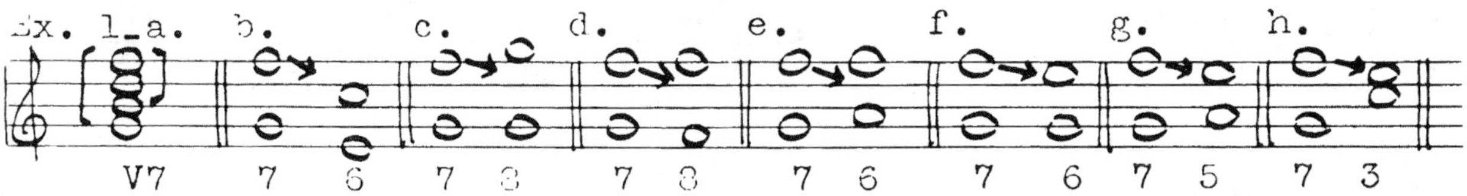

The resolution tendencies of the tritone have already been pointed out, (p. 28, sec. 7). Partial resolutions, Ex. 2-a, b, and c, will be found in the treatment of secondary sevenths, but almost never in the dominant seventh chord. Ex. 2-d and its inversion 2-e provide the only really satisfactory resolutions, and as they both imply either I or VI, these chords are clearly designated as the normal chords of resolution.

2 **Resolution to the Tonic.** In a four note chord, no doubling is necessary. The resolution of the dissonances in the dominant seventh chord results in a tonic triad with three roots, one third and no fifth, which is usually perfectly satisfactory, as there can seldom be any doubt as to what chord is intended. Frequently, however, the fifth is omitted from the V 7 chord, and its root doubled so that the chord of resolution may appear complete. Ex. 3-b. Any tone may appear in the soprano, the common tone being obviously the weakest from the melodic standpoint. In Ex. 3-c the leading tone, *in an inner voice,* is allowed to skip down to provide harmonic completeness in the chord of resolution. The resolution to I 6 in Ex. 3-d is thoroughly unsatisfactory.

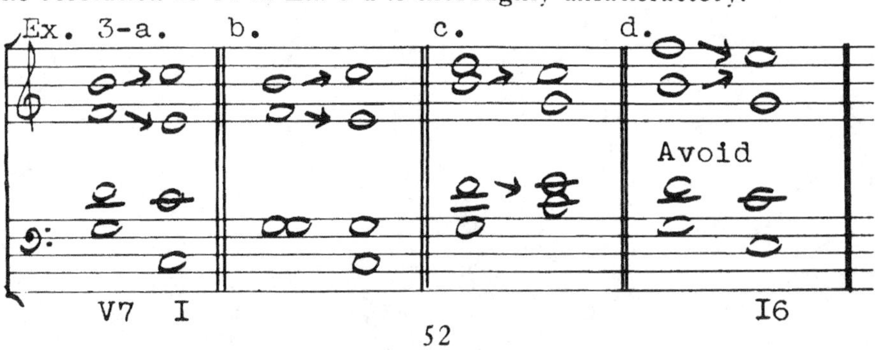

3 **Resolution to the Submediant.** This is frequently called the *deceptive resolution,* because the normal tendency of V into I is thus evaded. By this process of "detouring", the length of the harmonic phrase may be considerably extended. It occurs most frequently when the leading tone is in the soprano, in which case the latter tone invariably follows its normal tendency into the keytone, even though the result, in minor keys, is a doubled major third, Ex. 4-a and b. Even though the leading tone is in an inner voice, the resolution in Ex. 4-c is less satisfactory than the normal one. Under no circumstances should the dominant seventh be resolved to an *inversion* of the submediant, Ex. 4-d. Placing the keytone in the bass nullifies the whole purpose of the deceptive resolution, which was to avoid this tone.

The addition of the seventh to the dominant triad with resultant tritone greatly intensifies its dominant effect. With its resolution chord (I) it contains all the tones of the scale except the tonally unimportant sixth scale-step, and the progression V_7 - I firmly establishes the tonal primacy of the I chord, unless there are other disturbing factors.

It may be noted that the leading tone triad is nothing more than an incomplete dominant seventh, functioning in all cases as though the dominant chord-root were actually present.

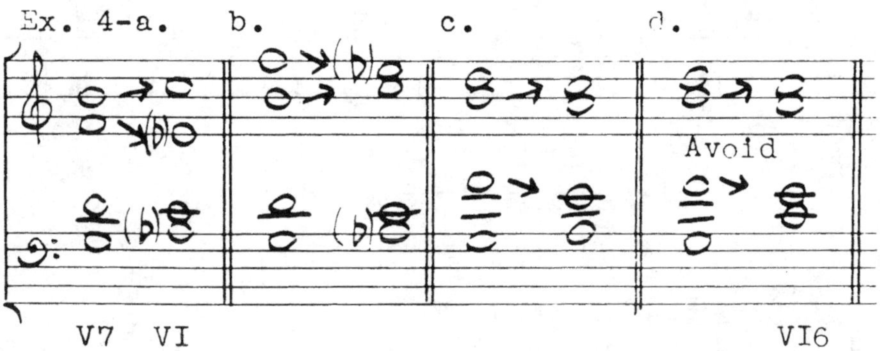

Exercises: Add the inner parts to the following diaphonies; the sign * indicates a dominant seventh chord. Give complete figuring.

2.

3.

4.

CHAPTER XIV

THE INVERSIONS OF THE DOMINANT SEVENTH CHORD

The inversions are three in number, and are best identified by reference to the figuring used in a figured bass. Counting from the bass tone upwards, and omitting irrelevant duplications, we obtain six-five for the first inversion, four-three for the second and four-two for the third. Note that in the close position of any seventh chord inversion, the root is always the *upper of two tones on adjacent degrees of the scale.*

While other resolutions are possible, the basic one to the tonic is the only one to be considered here. Since inversions of seventh chords seldom appear incomplete, no tone may be doubled, and none omitted, and the soprano and bass tones are never the same. There are thus three available soprano tones for each inversion.

1 **The Six-Five.** As the leading tone is the bass tone, the only available resolution is the fundamental tonic chord. The tritone resolution is always normal, and the chord seventh, whether above or below the root, always moves stepwise downward, Ex. 1-a, b, c.

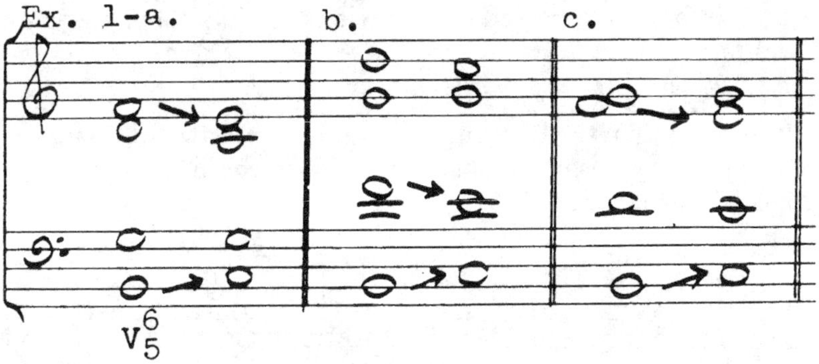

2 **The Four-Three,** in which the tritone is not exposed in the bass, has somewhat more freedom of movement. Aside from its normal resolution to I, Ex. 2-a, b, c, it may also resolve to I 6 Ex. 2-d, e. In Ex. 2-d the chord seventh (F) being in an inner voice does not resolve by falling, but moves up to avoid a bad doubling in the chord of resolution. In Ex. 2-e the same process is noted, with resultant consecutive fifths, diminished to perfect, which are sanctioned in this progression by general usage. The four-three chord in this example is really a passing chord, all the moving tones being either passing or returning tones. This is the only normal case of a dominant seventh resolving *up.* Otherwise it invariably resolves *down.*

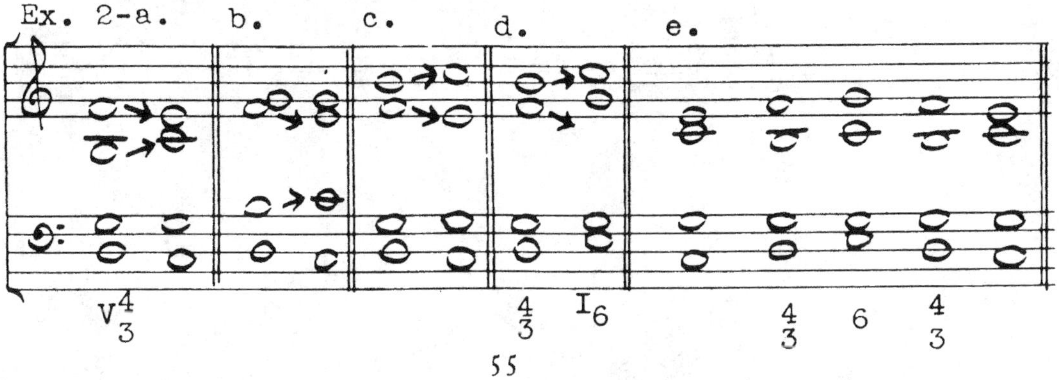

3 **The Four-Two** again exposes the tritone in the bass. In this form it must resolve by *stepwise expansion,* so that the only available chord of resolution is I 6 If the root or fifth occur in the soprano, they are free to leap up a perfect fourth, Ex. 3-c, d, and this progression provides a good solution for the problems in melody harmonization which always occur at points where the melody leaps up a fourth.

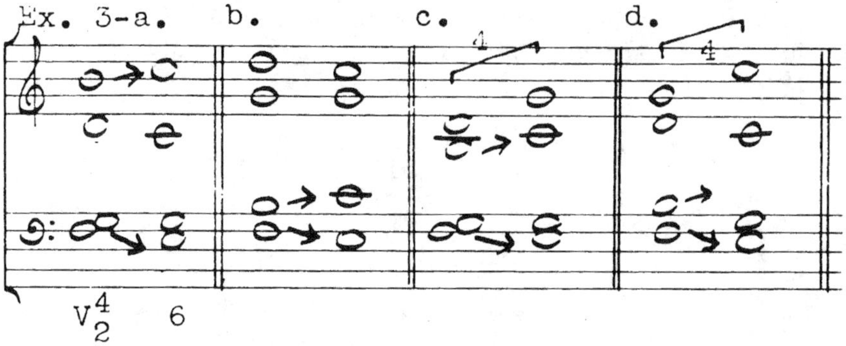

4 The principal value of the dominant seventh inversions derives from the large amount of melodic cohesion which results in the part writing, since nearly all the parts move stepwise. Indeed, every tone of a diatonic melody except the sixth scale-tone may be harmonized by one of these chords and its resolution, and from the harmonic standpoint whole pages of the classic masters, and especially Beethoven, contain little else. Inversions provide at best only weak or partial cadences; their principal use is at the beginning and in the course of phrases, but never at the end, if a strong and conclusive cadence is desired. Expressed in terms of the diaphony, they make possible the use of the major second and minor seventh as well as the tritone on strong beats, always assuming that a proper resolution is provided for these dissonances.

Exercises: Add a bass part, with complete figuring, to the following melodies. After these diaphonies have been approved by the instructor, fill in the inner parts. The sign * indicates a dominant seventh chord or inversion.

5.

6.

7.

8.

CHAPTER XV

EXTENDED DOMINANT HARMONIES

By extending upwards the series of thirds above the dominant it is possible to obtain a theoretical chord of the *dominant thirteenth,* which is in effect a composite of the seventh chords on the dominant, leading tone, supertonic and subdominant. From this series certain useful combinations are derived.

Ex. 1

1 **The Dominant Ninth Chord,** containing five tones, cannot be completely represented in four part harmony, and was first given prominence by the romantic composers of the nineteenth century, who were mostly instrumental writers. Its uses in choral style are very limited.

Strictly speaking, a ninth chord is uninvertible, since the inversion of a ninth produces a seventh. Aside from the fundamental position of the ninth chord, however, it is possible, while still retaining the ninth uninverted, to sound the third or the seventh below the root, thus obtaining two pseudo-inversions. In four part writing the fifth is always omitted; in five or more parts another "inversion" with the fifth in the bass is possible.

Ex. 2-a. b. c. d. e. f.

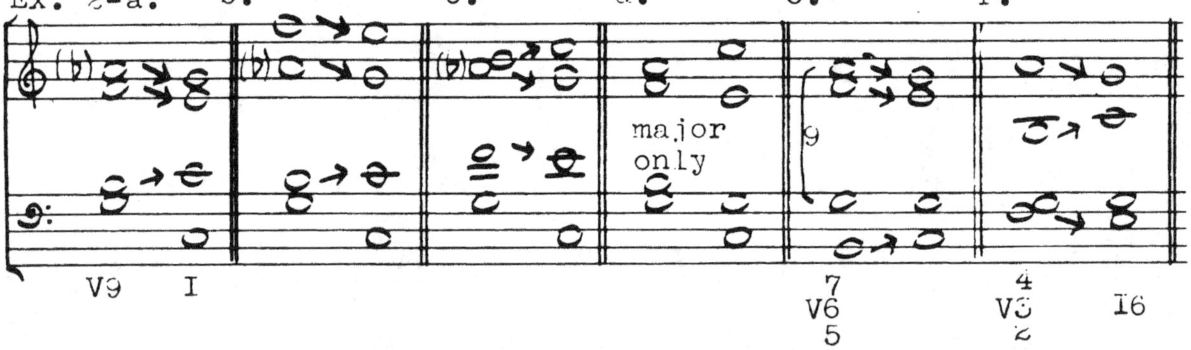

In resolving to the tonic chord, the ninth usually falls stepwise in parallel motion with the seventh. On occasion, however, it may leap up a third to the keytone, in which case the leading tone, in an inner voice, leaps down to supply the missing fifth of the tonic, Ex. 2-d. Note that three figures are necessary to express the "inversions". In minor keys the interval of the diminished seventh or augmented second is introduced between the ninth and the leading tone. This makes the resolution in Ex. 2-d unavailable, but all others are equally good.

2 **The Dominant Eleventh Chord** is of limited usefulness, because of the sharp tonal disagreement between the keytone and the leading tone, both of which are theoretical members of the chord though the leading tone is usually omitted. In four parts it has the effect of a dominant chord with leading tone suspension, Ex. 3-a. Late romantic and modern composers have used it extensively.

3 **The Dominant Thirteenth Chord** may be described as a combination of the mediant sixth superimposed upon the dominant seventh, Ex. 4-a. Added harmonic tension is produced by the major seventh which occurs between the seventh and the thirteenth of the chord; this tension is somewhat softened if the minor thirteenth is used, Ex. 4-b. As a rule the thirteenth is left unresolved, leaping down a third, Ex. 4-c. The chord is obviously uninvertible, and will be more fully discussed in Chapter XXX, (Five-part writing).

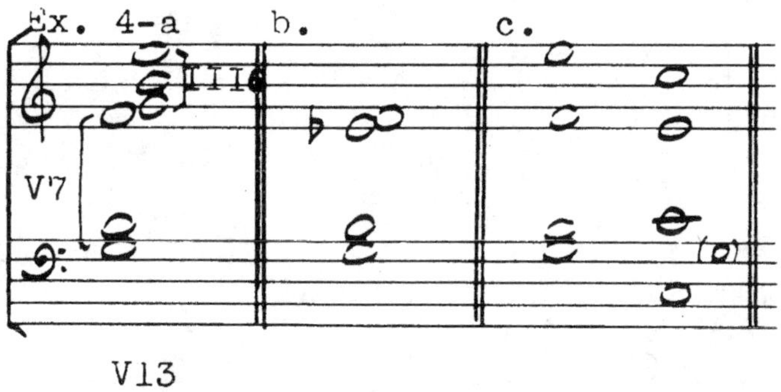

4 **The Leading Tone Seventh Chord** is by far the most useful of all the chords derived from the extended dominant series. Note that in major keys it presents the exact intervallic structure of the dominant seventh chord by inversion, that is, counting downward from the upper tone it consists of a major third, perfect fifth and minor seventh, Ex. 5-a. It may also be thought of as a chord consisting of two interlocking fifths, the *lower* of which is a tritone, Ex. 5-b; (in the dominant seventh chord the *upper* fifth is the tritone.) It is convenient to refer to chords of this type as *half-diminished,* as distinct from the fully diminished seventh chords which consist of two interlocking tritones. Either type of leading tone seventh chord actually functions as an incomplete dominant ninth chord, its discords resolving exactly as though the dominant root were actually present.

It always resolves to the tonic, as any other resolution would immediately change its *function.* As it consists exclusively of "neighbor" tones of the tonic triad, care must be used in its resolution to avoid objectionable consecutive fifths, Ex. 5-c. The usual result is a doubled third in the chord of resolution, even if this be major, Ex. 5-d, though with the third in the soprano this doubling may be avoided, Ex. 5-e.

5 **Inversions of the Leading Tone Seventh Chord.** The normal resolution of L^6_5 is into I_6, Ex. 6-a, though this results in a doubled major third in the latter chord, which sounds better if it can be approached and left stepwise by contrary motion, Ex. 6-b. A possible resolution into the fundamental tonic is shown in Ex. 6-c.

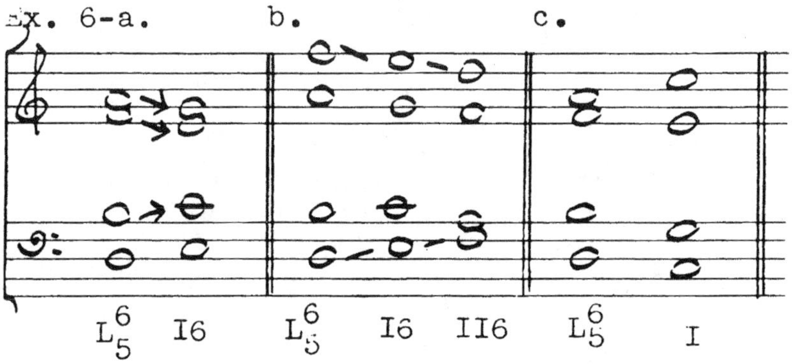

The L^4_3 also resolves to I_6 with doubled third, Ex. 7-a. In this case the doubled third may be avoided by a downward fourth-leap in the bass, Ex. 7-b, or an upward fourth-leap in the soprano, Ex. 7-c. Several rearrangements of the upper parts, not shown in the examples, are obviously possible.

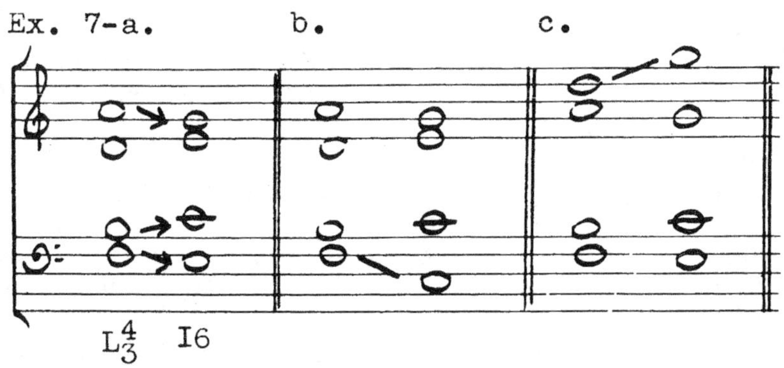

The L^4_2 resolving theoretically into I^6_4 is of little practical value, Ex. 8-a, as its bass tone sounds so much like a neighbor tone of the dominant root that it generally functions as such, Ex. 8-b.

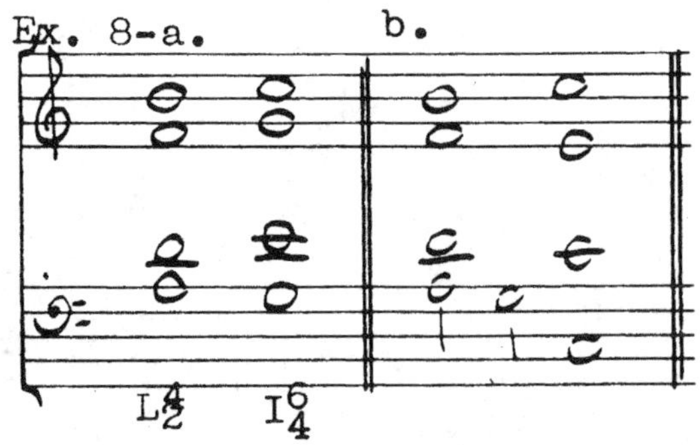

6 **The Diminished Seventh Chord.** The leading tone seventh chord in minor keys has a diminished seventh as well as a diminished fifth. Although derived from the extended dominant series, it has in many cases just the opposite *function* from that of the dominant seventh chord. The latter chord is the most positive of all tonal determinants, while the *diminished seventh chord* in many cases serves to obscure or nullify any feeling of tonality. An examination of its interval structure makes the reason for this apparent. It is made up exclusively of superimposed minor thirds, and has therefore the ambiguous quality of any chord made up of *equal intervals;* and since both its fifths are diminished, it contains two interlocking tritones, with their strong but contradictory resolution tendencies. Some of the possibilities are suggested in Ex. 10.

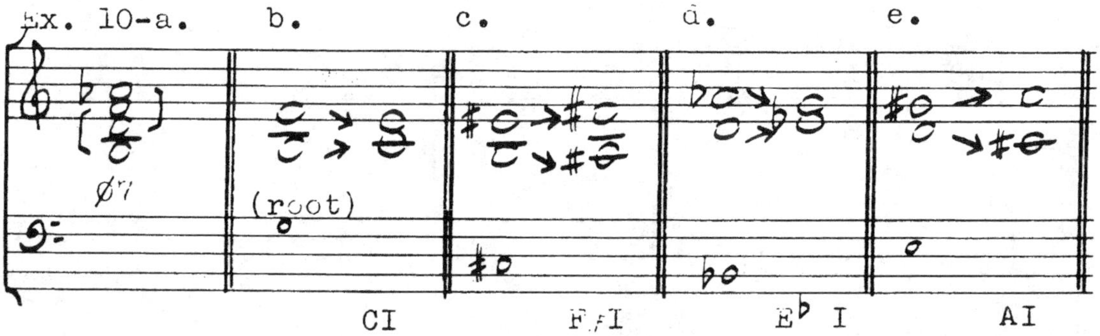

Through the use of enharmonic spelling the tritones in the *diminished seventh chord* on B appear to have tendencies towards three keys remote from C, — F sharp, E flat and A. These are only the most obvious of many others. Since the implied root can only be determined by the context, it cannot be indicated by a degree number or letter; we shall designate it with the sign ø7.

Any minor third, enharmonically spelled, becomes an augmented second. This produces a purely theoretical change in the position of the leading tone, with consequent change in tonal tendency, Ex. 11-a. These changes in notation are only apprehended by the listener *after* hearing the chord of resolution. The inversions, though convenient to indicate in analysis, *do not actually exist in sound,* as the same intervallic structure is merely reproduced at higher or lower pitches. Ex. 11-b.

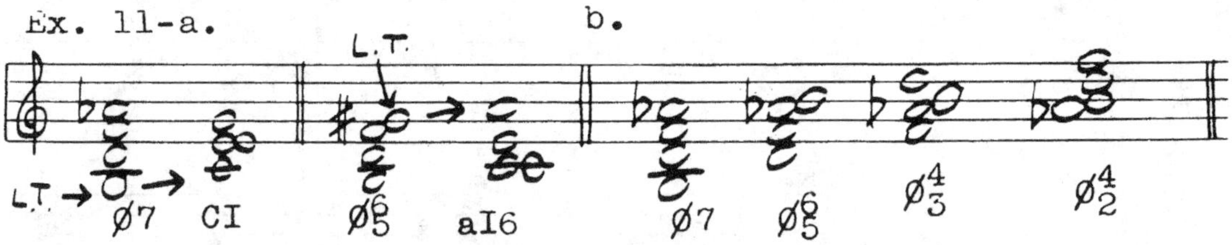

When based upon the leading tone, the *diminished seventh chord* resolves in exactly the same way as the leading tone seventh in major keys. Other uses of the diminished seventh will be reserved for later discussion. As both its fifths are diminished, it may be approached by similar motion of all four voices, Ex. 12-a, but its proper resolution will nearly always result in a doubled third. The resolutions involving fourth leaps in the bass or soprano, Ex. 12-b and c, are sometimes effective.

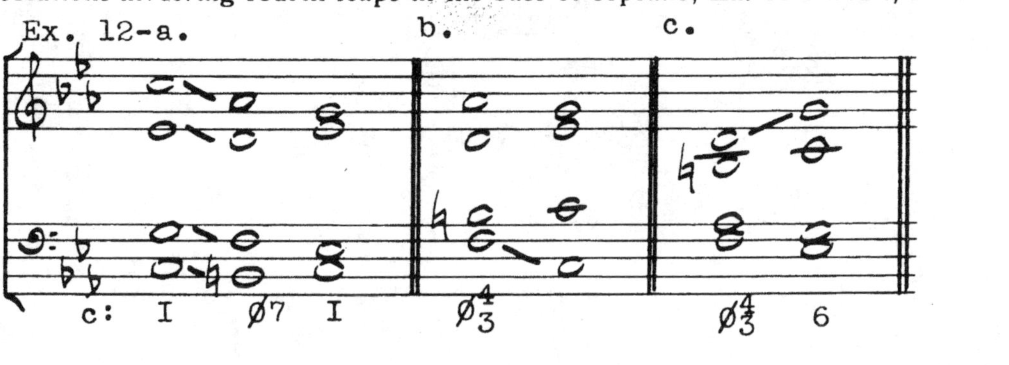

Although its original form is derived from the minor mode, the *diminished seventh chord* is freely used in major keys, where it is formed by lowering the seventh above the leading tone (sixth scale-step) a semitone. Used in this way, it forms a type of chromatic embellishing chord, about which more will be said in a later chapter. The resolution chord, in many cases, will have a doubled *major* third, which is almost invariably preferable to a resolution involving the succession of two fifths in the order diminished to perfect.

GROUP I Extended Dominant Harmonies

GROUP II Diminished Seventh Chord and inversions

CHAPTER XVI

THE SUPERTONIC SEVENTH CHORD

1 Second only in tonal value and importance to the dominant seventh chord is that based upon the supertonic. When the seventh is added to the supertonic triad, the result is a combination of the subdominant and supertonic triads, containing the melodically valuable second scale tone added to the tonally strong triad on the fourth degree. Indeed, the chord may be thought of as a pair of interlocking fifths, Ex. 1-b, of which the primary fifth F - C is much closer to the key center than the secondary fifth D - A, so that the F tends to be heard as the root and the D as an added third below it. This tendency is greatly increased in minor keys, where the lower fifth in the chord is a tritone, and the resulting intervallic structure makes it a half-diminished type, indistinguishable in sound from a leading tone seventh chord, Ex. 1-c. As the tritone is without root feeling, other factors in the chord have to supply this lack, and it is natural to assume that the root of the perfect fifth is in fact the fundamental of the chord. The function, therefore, of the supertonic seventh chord is *subdominant;* like the leading tone seventh chord it presents the picture of the dominant seventh chord *by inversion,* Ex. 2, and the strongest possible definition of tonality is produced by the progression II_7 - V_7 - I.

2 **The Supertonic Six-Five** is the most useful of all the positions of this chord. It is in fact a subdominant triad with added sixth above the root, and has sometimes been referred to as the "chord of the added sixth"; the melodically important second scale-step appears in an upper voice, and the harmonically important subdominant root in the bass. In minor keys the added melodic tension of the tritone is also introduced, Ex. 3.

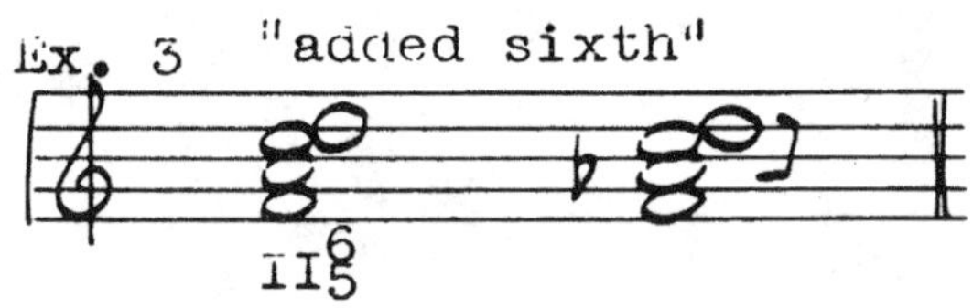

3 **Resolution.** The resolution of the supertonic seventh chord and its inversions offers little difficulty. With unimportant exceptions, the chord of resolution is always the dominant, Ex. 4-a. The seventh, in whatever voice it occurs, falls stepwise to the leading tone; the fifth, whether or not it is diminished, resolves stepwise down to the dominant root. The third is often used to prepare the seventh of the dominant, in which case the dominant seventh chord will omit its fifth. Ex. 4-b.

The resolution of II $^{6}_{5}$ requires no further comment, Ex. 4-c. The second inversion, II $^{4}_{3}$, is much less frequently used than the II $^{6}_{5}$, but equally easy to handle, Ex. 4-d. The third inversion, II $^{4}_{2}$, will resolve either to V $_{6}$ or to V $^{6}_{5}$, and is therefore seldom used in complete cadences; it most often occurs at the beginning of an harmonic sentence, directly following the initial tonic chord as in the first Prelude of the *Well Tempered Clavier* (J. S. Bach).

The supertonic seventh chord in fundamental position, and in its first and second, but *not* its third inversion may resolve into the tonic six-four chord before V in the cadence. The examples given are equally good in major or minor keys.

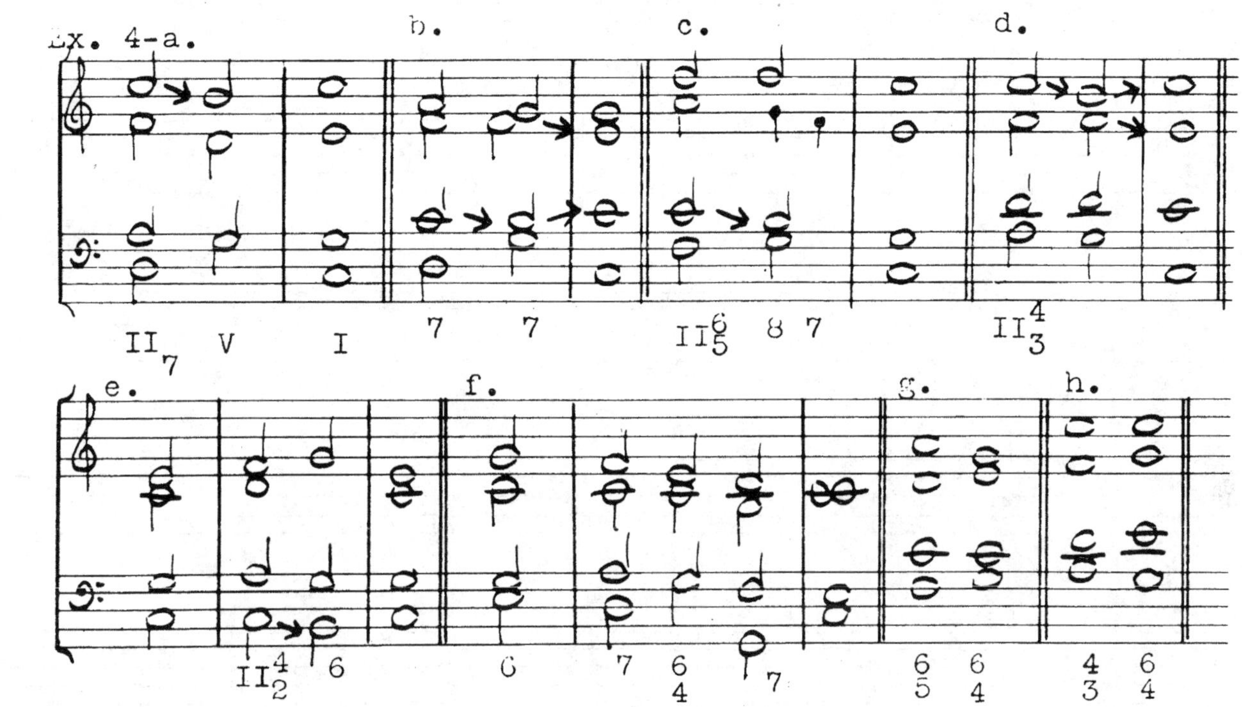

Supertonic Seventh Chord and Inversions

4.

e
4 3
(6 4)
V

5.

6.

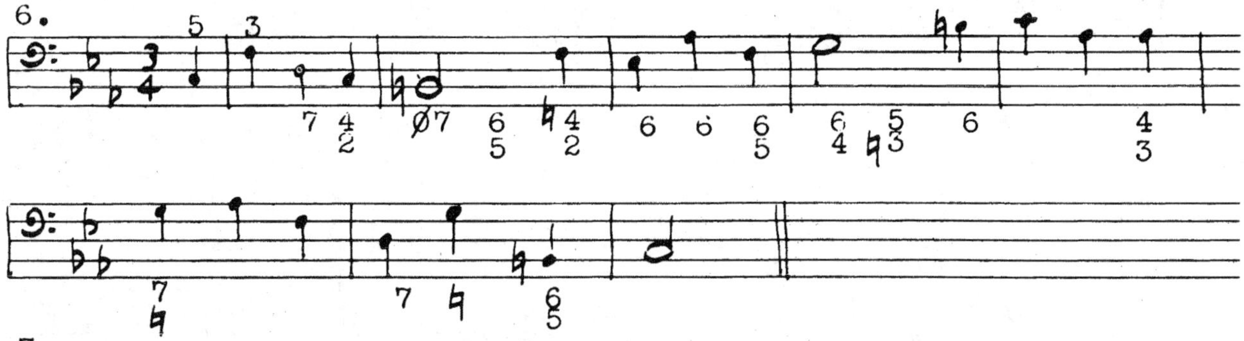
5 3
7 4 2 ø7 6 5 ♮ 4 2 6 6 6 5 6 4 ♮ 5 3 6 4 3
7 ♮ 7 ♮ 6 5

7.

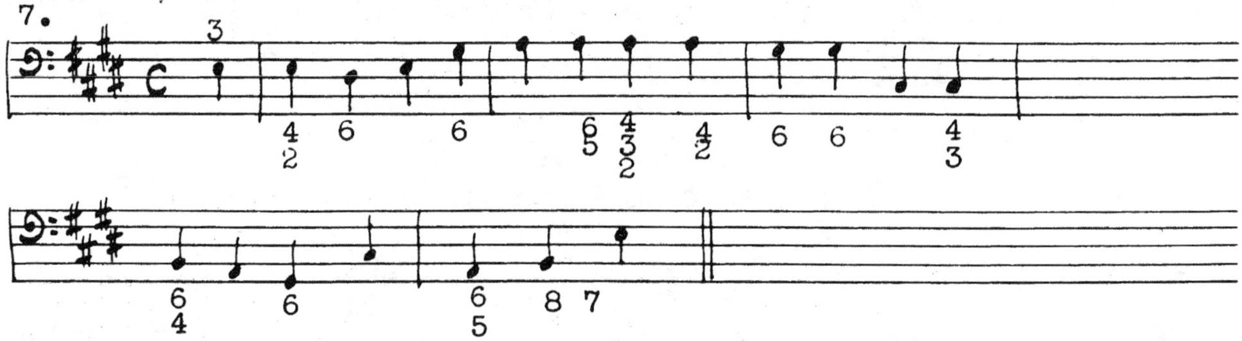
3
4 2 6 6 6 5 4 3 2 4 2 6 6 4 3
6 4 6 6 5 8 7

CHAPTER XVII

OTHER DIATONIC SEVENTH CHORDS

1 **Classification of Seventh Chords.** In the classification of seventh chords it is important to differentiate clearly between the *type* of chord and its *function* in an harmonic phrase or sentence. By type we refer to the intervallic structure of a chord. There are five types of seventh chord:

1 Major: a major seventh added to a major triad
2 Minor: a minor seventh added to a minor triad
3 Dominant: a minor seventh added to a major triad
4 Half-diminished: a minor seventh added to a diminished triad
5 Diminished: a diminished seventh added to a diminished triad

Note that the first two types contain no tritone, and consist of *interlocking perfect fifths*, type 1 at the interval of a major third, and type 2 at the minor third. The remaining three types all contain tritones; the dominant has a tritone as its upper fifth, the half-diminished at its lower fifth, and the diminished seventh chord consists of two interlocking tritones at the interval of a minor third.

The diminished seventh chord is not properly speaking a diatonic seventh chord, since it requires an accidental (the leading tone) to make it in its most usual form, as leading tone seventh in minor keys. However the leading tone is an essential part of all dominant harmonies; its use in other chords, such as the tonic or mediant seventh chords in minor keys, referred to later in this chapter, partakes more of the nature of chromatic alteration.

2 **Function of Seventh Chords.** By *function* we refer to the relationship of a chord to others in the tonal scheme of a phrase or sentence; in other words, type refers to what a chord *is,* and function to what it *does*. Of the five types, the only one whose tonal function is predetermined is the dominant seventh, which always produces dominant feeling no matter how irregularly it may be resolved. Major seventh chords occur as I_7 and IV_7 in major keys, and as III_7 and VI_7 in minor keys. Minor seventh chords occur on II, III and VI in major keys, and I and IV in minor keys. Half-diminished seventh chords occur as L_7 in major and II_7 in minor keys. The diminished seventh chord has a great variety of uses, but the only one under consideration in the present chapter is that on the leading tone. It should be noted that the leading tone diminished seventh is very frequently used in major keys, where it is produced by lowering the sixth scale-tone in the leading tone seventh chord.

3 **Resolution.** All seventh chords except IV_7 may resolve in Class I, the seventh falling stepwise, with upward fourth-leap of roots, Ex. 1. The Class III resolution, stepwise in all parts, is normal for IV_7, and may be used for all others except VI_7, Ex. 2. The strong natural resolution tendency of the leading tone may cause the I_7 to resolve in Class II, Ex. 3, and this exceptional treatment is occasionally used with IV_7, Ex. 3-c.

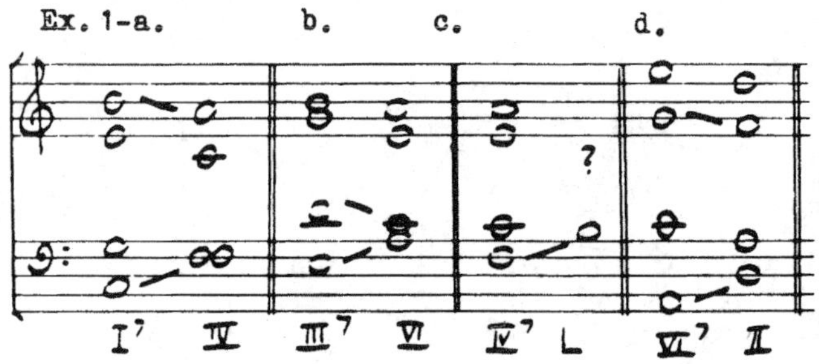

The Class I resolution of one seventh chord into another, following the pattern: II_7 - V_7 discussed in the preceding chapter, is of excellent effect with nearly all the seventh chords, and the addition of a seventh to the leading tone triad makes the latter available as a chord of resolution for IV_7, Ex. 4-a and 4-b, (if one seventh chord can be said to "resolve" another). Since L_7, unlike the dominant seventh, may not omit its fifth, some rather unusual voice leading is necessary in order to supply it. Any of the seventh chords may also be connected in Class II or Class III; the IV_7 is the one most frequently treated in this way, Ex. 4-c and d.

4 **Treatment in Minor Keys.** In using these chords in minor keys, account must be taken of the effect upon them and their resolutions of the minor scales, and particularly of the alterations of the sixth and seventh scale-tones. In this respect the II_7 and L_7 have been thoroughly covered in preceding chapters. The seventh chord on the subtonic (VII_7) is a dominant seventh of the relative major key, and should not be used unless modulation is intended.

The natural upward tendency of the leading tone, if present in the I_7, causes it to resolve invariably in Class II, Ex. 5-a. With unaltered seventh, the I_7 resolves in Class I, Ex. 5-b. The Class III resolution is not available for obvious reasons.

The presence of the leading tone in the III_7 causes it to resolve, like the I_7, in Class II, Ex. 6-a. The Class I resolution, Ex. 6-b, is also possible. In the usual harmonization of the descending scale it resolves in Class III, Ex. 6-c. The resolution in Ex. 6-d, while possible, is awkward.

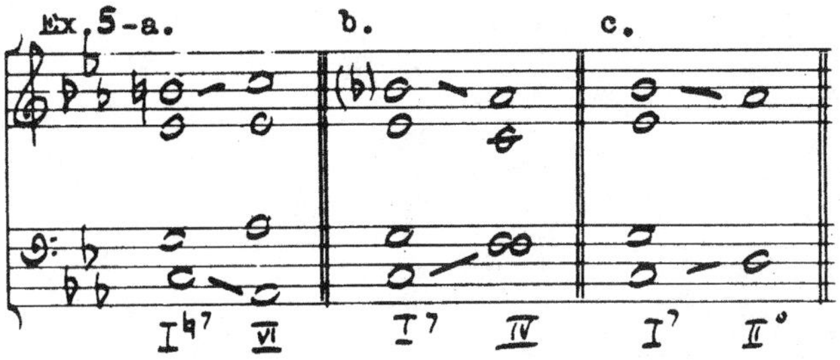

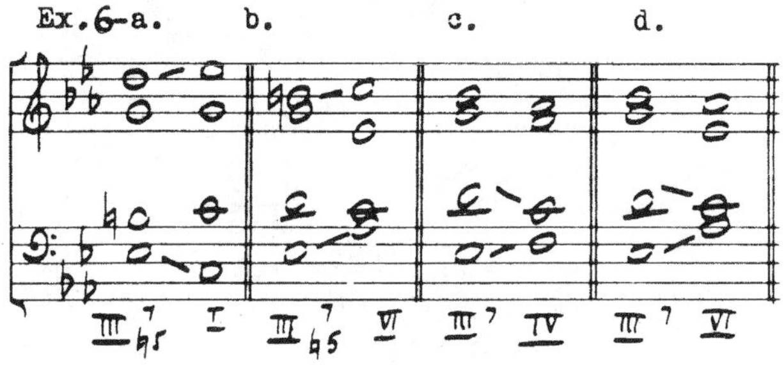

The IV 7 in minor keys resolves only in Class III, Ex. 7-a. Ex. 7-b illustrates an interesting use of the ascending melodic minor scale often used by J. S. Bach, in which the raised sixth scale-tone produces a dominant type seventh chord on IV. The distribution of the raised six and seventh scale-tones between two different parts should otherwise be carefully avoided.

The seventh chord with minor third on the dominant is *not* a dominant seventh, but is of excellent effect in the resolution to VI, Ex. 7-c. The major seventh chord on the submediant normally resolves only in Class II, Ex. 7-d, the other resolutions being obviously unsatisfactory; as a half-diminished chord on the *raised sixth* scale-tone it may resolve in Class III, Ex. 7-g.

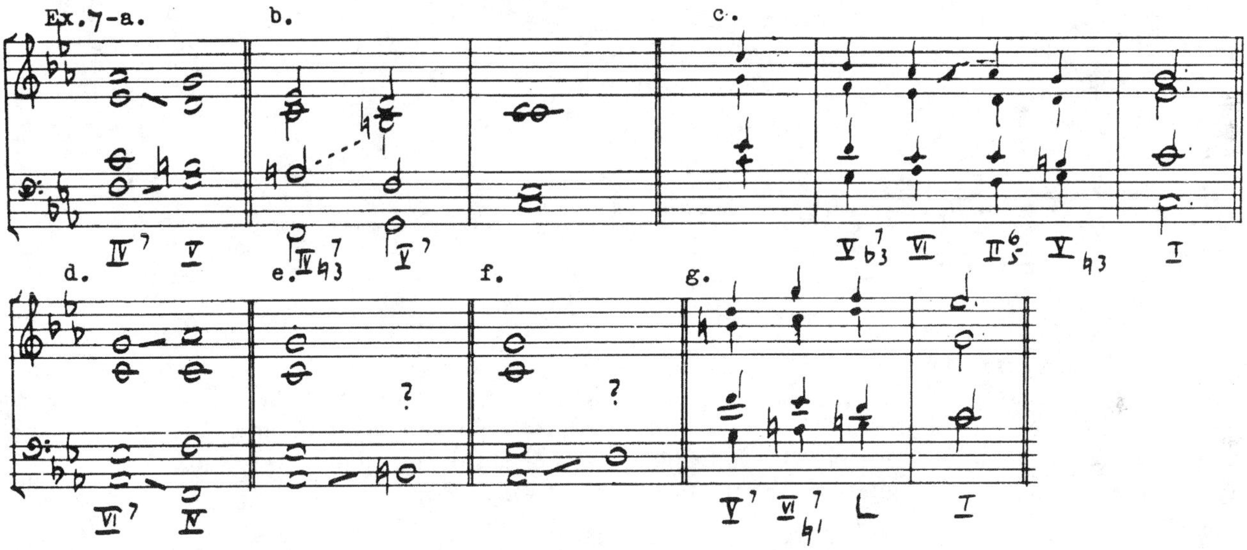

5 **Inversions of Diatonic Seventh Chords.** An inversion of a seventh chord may be resolved in three ways: into a triad, a sixth chord, or another seventh chord. Taking the inversions of the tonic seventh as typical, Table I illustrates the various resolutions into triads and sixth chords. The last inversion with the seventh in the bass is almost invariably the result of a passing tone, Ex. d. Most of these resolutions are equally good in minor keys. The student should construct for himself a similar table for the inversions of other seventh chords, noting carefully resolutions to be avoided because of augmented leaps, or resulting diminished triads. Notice that in all Class II progressions in this table the sevenths fall instead of rising.

TABLE I

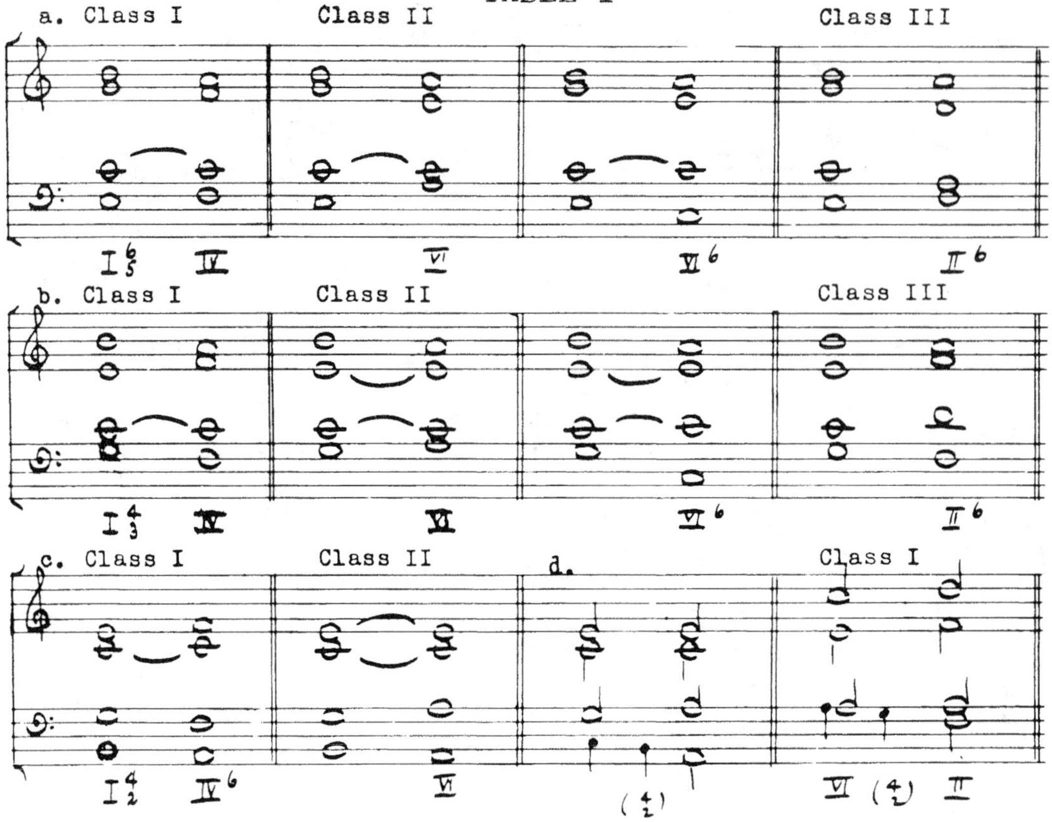

In resolving an inversion of a seventh chord into another seventh chord, only Class I or Class III progressions are available. In Class II there are *three* common tones, and the single moving part invariably sounds like a neighbor tone and its resolution. Table II shows the available resolutions of the inversions of I7. Note that in Class I progressions seven resolves to four-three, and six-five to four-two, and vice versa. The Class III resolution in Ex. d results in parallel fifths, which may be avoided by inverting the parts, Ex. e and f.

TABLE II

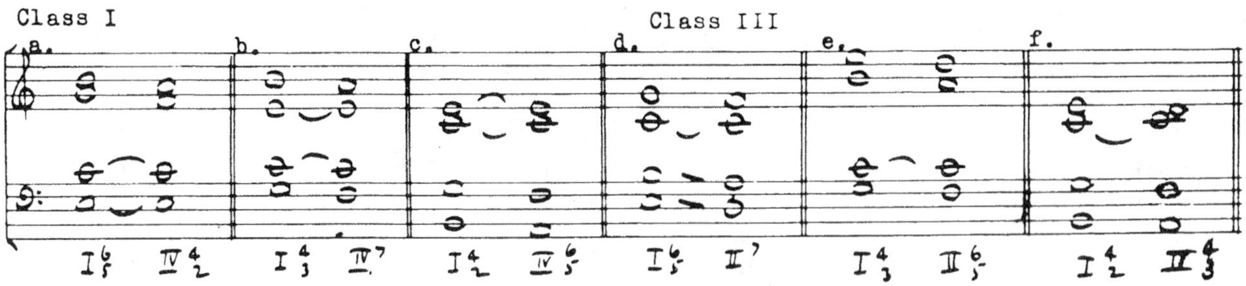

6 **Seventh Chords in Sequence.** Patterns for sequential treatment are readily constructed out of a pair of seventh chords, and such sequences abound in the works of such masters as Corelli, Handel and J. S. Bach. The most useful patterns are derived from Class I progressions, the roots moving alternately up a fourth and down a fifth. Alternate chords may be triads, or the sequence pattern may consist of a continuous chain of sevenths, either in root position or inversion.

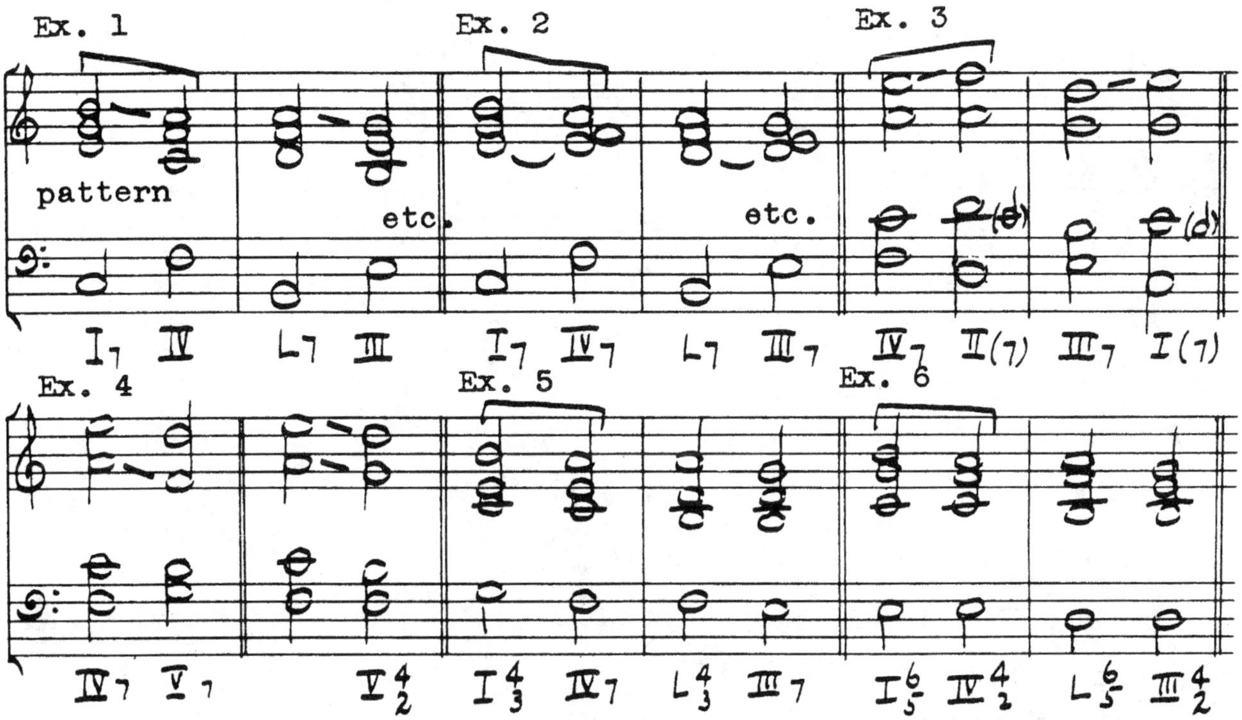

In all Class I sequences *when the melody moves stepwise down the root moves up a fourth, and when the melody remains stationary the root moves down a fifth.*

If the pattern contains fundamental seventh chords, *alternate fifths are omitted,* Ex. 2.

Sequences in Class II, Ex. 3, and Class III, Ex. 4, though possible, are rather rare, as are any patterns in which the general movement is upward instead of down.

Where inversions are involved, the positions alternate: that is, root position is followed or preceded by four-three, Ex. 5, and the six-five by the four-two, Ex. 6.

Sequences of sevenths provide excellent material for keyboard practice. The student should experiment with all possible positions of the soprano in the sequence pattern, and should transpose the exercises to all keys.

GROUP I

GROUP II, with inversions

KEYBOARD EXERCISES, Seventh chords in sequence

1.

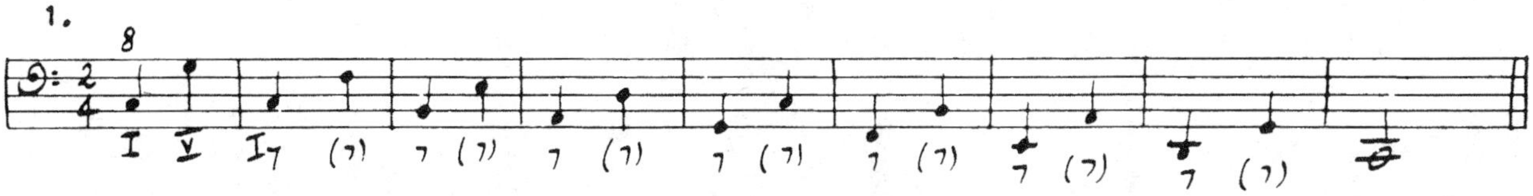

2.

3.

4.

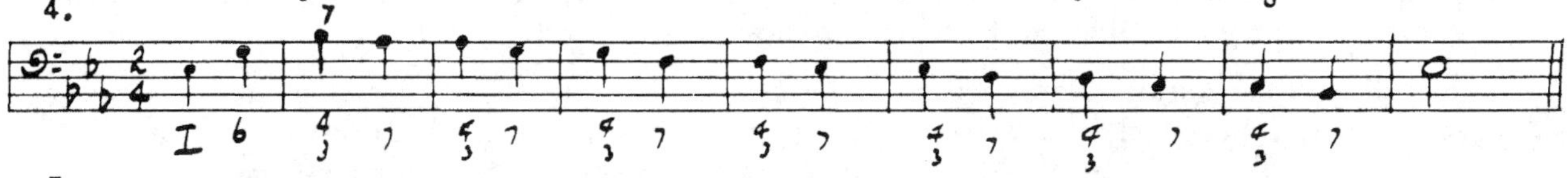

5.

CHAPTER XVIII

MODULATION BY COMMON CHORDS

One of the simplest ways of avoiding monotony in the writing of music is through modulation. A key center having been established by the use of one or more cadences in the principal key, variety is obtained by changing the key center through the process known as modulation. This may be effected in a number of different ways, of which one of the simplest and most useful is that of modulation by common chords.

We have seen in a preceding chapter (Chap. IV, Sec. 2) that all chords in a given key have one or more tones in common with other chords in the same key. Similarly, a chord which occurs unaltered in two or more different keys is "common" to them all.

Recalling that major triads occur as the One, Four, and Five chords in major keys, and the Three, Six, and Seven chords in minor keys; that minor triads occur as the Two, Three, and Six chords in major keys, and the One, Four, and Five chords in minor keys; and that diminished triads occur as the Leading Tone chord in major keys and the Two chord in minor keys, we can construct the following table of Common Chords:

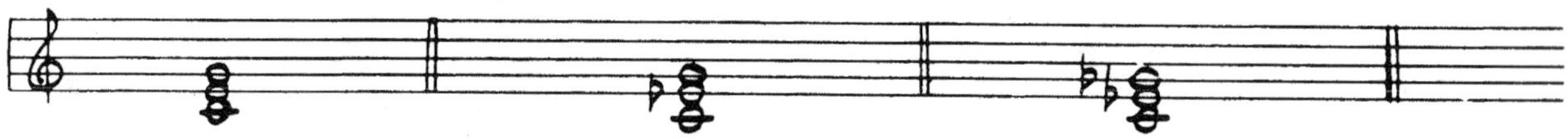

C major I	B flat major II	D flat major I.
G major IV	A flat major III	B flat minor II.
F major V	E flat major VI	
A minor III	C minor I	
E minor VI	G minor IV	
D minor VII	F minor V	

Note the exclusive use, in the foregoing table, of the unaltered *natural minor scale*. As already noted in chapter X, the artificially raised leading tone is principally used in cadences.

The modulations most frequently made by common chords are those to related keys. The related keys of a given major key are those whose tonic chords are represented by the triads Two to Six inclusive in that key. Thus the related keys of C major are D minor, E minor, F major, G major, and A minor.

The related keys of a given minor key are those whose tonic triads are represented by the triads Three to Seven inclusive in that key. Thus the related keys of A minor are C major, D minor, E minor, F major, and G major.

> *Note*: The common appearance of the lowered sixth degree in major keys has already been noted. Obviously the chord c-e-g is also the Dominant of F minor, which is to be considered as related to C major. Similarly the A minor triad is of frequent occurrence as IV in E major, and the latter key may be considered related to A minor.

While modulation may take place at almost any point in a phrase, we will consider at present only those modulations which take the tonic chord of the first key as their starting point. The chord c-e-g sounded by itself gives us no hint as to which of the various chords indicated in the table above it represents. The chord which follows it may or may not define its relationship more clearly. In Ex. 1-a we cannot tell whether the progression is in C major or F major; in 1-b it might be in either C major, F major, or A minor. But in example 1-c there is no doubt; the F# clearly shows that the first chord must be considered the IV of G.

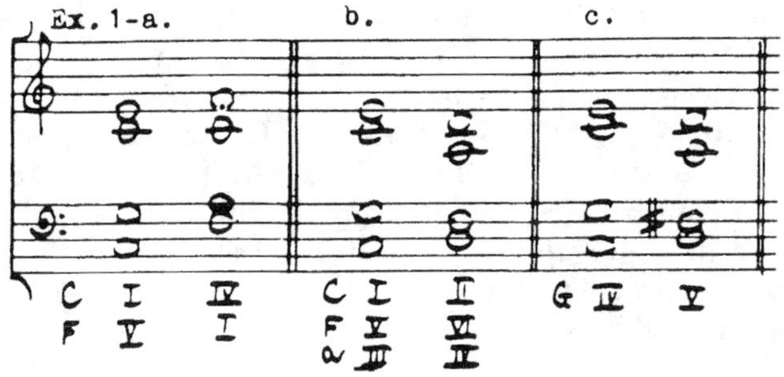

It is not sufficient, however, to add a tonic chord in G major and say that a modulation to G has been effected. The use of the so-called "embellishing" or "neighbor" dominant and diminished seventh chords within a given key is extremely common and will be fully discussed later. Observe in Ex. 2-a that the F# in the first measure is immediately contradicted by the F♮ in the second measure. There is no feeling of modulation, and the II seven with raised third is to be considered a neighbor dominant seventh of C major V. In Ex. 2-b, on the other hand, the modulation to G major is clearly indicated by the complete cadence in G which follows the altered chord.

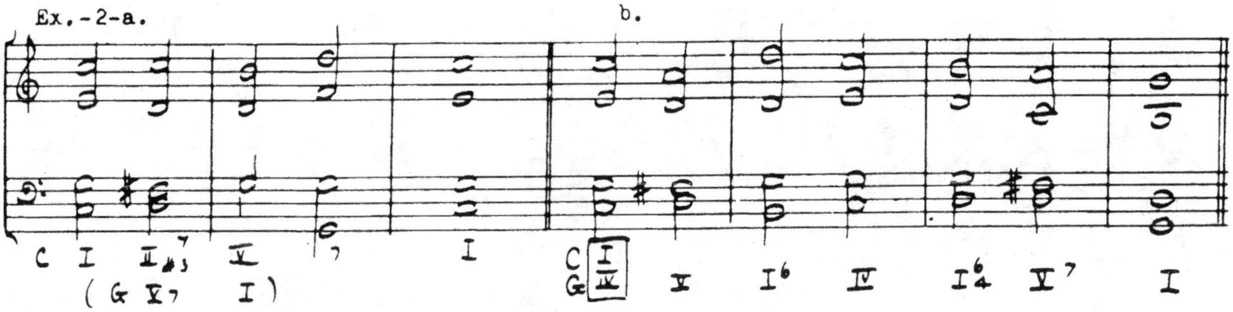

Note: Actual modulation does not occur unless a new key center is definitely established, usually by the use of a complete cadence in the new key.

The student should carefully avoid a redundant double full cadence as illustrated in Ex. 3-a. This may be done either by the use of a deceptive resolution, Ex. 3-b, or by the use of inversions. The last inversion of the dominant seventh is particularly useful in this connection, resolving as it does into I_6, Ex. 3-c and 3-d. Other inversions of the V_7 may also be used, Ex. 3-e.

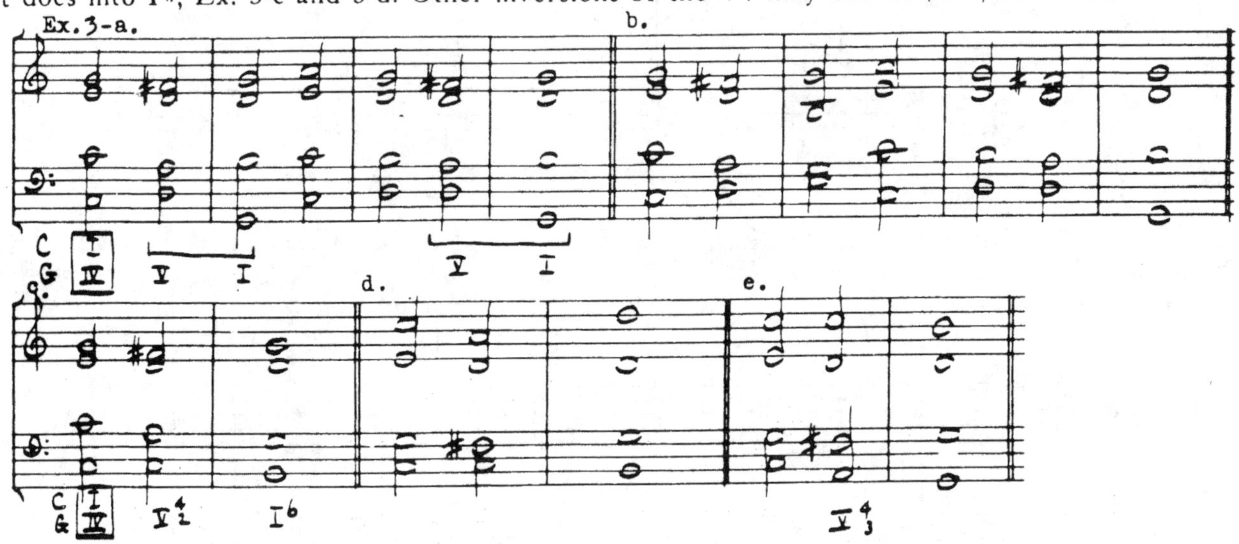

In modulating to the subdominant we find that the tonic chord of the first key is the dominant of the second. But, as already shown, on p. 75, Ex. 1-a, the mere sequence of these two chords does not clearly indicate the tonality. It is, therefore, best to repeat the first chord, adding to it a minor seventh, which clearly defines it as a dominant seventh (in major keys, of course; minor keys will be dealt with in turn). The resulting full cadence, which must be followed by a *complete* cadence in order to show that the V_7 is not merely an embellishing chord of IV, involves us in the difficulty of another redundant double full cadence. This may be avoided either by the use of inversions, or by a deceptive resolution. In Ex. 4-a the six-five inversion is used. In Ex. 4-b the four-two, which is preferable, because of the smooth bass line resulting. In Ex. 4-c the deceptive resolution is used.

The modulation to the relative minor, (review chapter X), is one of the most frequent, and all seven triads are common to both keys. In fact, it is hardly correct to speak of a "modulation" to the relative minor. The transition is readily effected through the progression $I-L_6$ in the major key, which represents $III-II_6$ in the minor, Ex. 5-a, or I-II in the major, corresponding to III-IV in the minor, Ex. 5-b.

The modulation to the mediant key, (relative minor of the dominant) may be made through the progression VI-IV, or better VI-II. The latter chord may be inverted, and is frequently a six-five. Ex. 6-b illustrates the use of the latter, approached by a passing four-two in the bass which is extremely smooth.

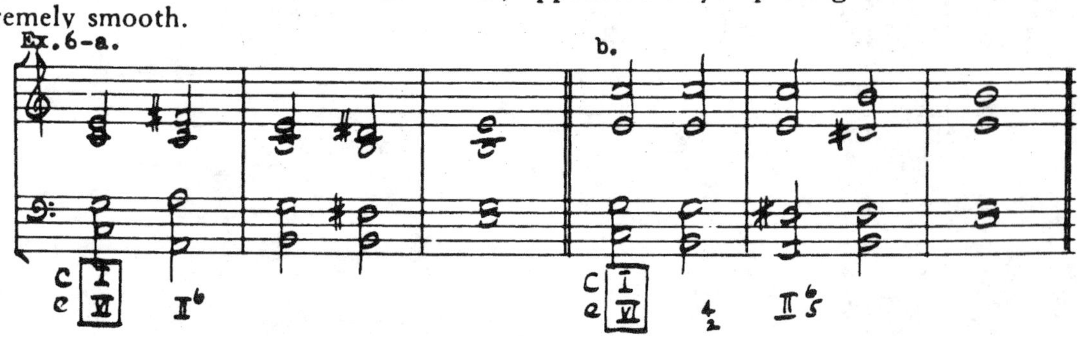

The modulation to the supertonic key, (relative minor of the subdominant), is the most difficult. In going from C major to D minor the effect of the C natural in the C major I must be cancelled before the C sharp of the V of D minor may be introduced. This is best done by the use of the IV or II 7 of the minor key, Ex. 7-a and b.

No further remarks are needed concerning the modulations from a minor key to its various related keys. Observe the use of a deceptive resolution (in one case with IV 6) in making the modulation from A minor to D minor, Ex. 8-e.

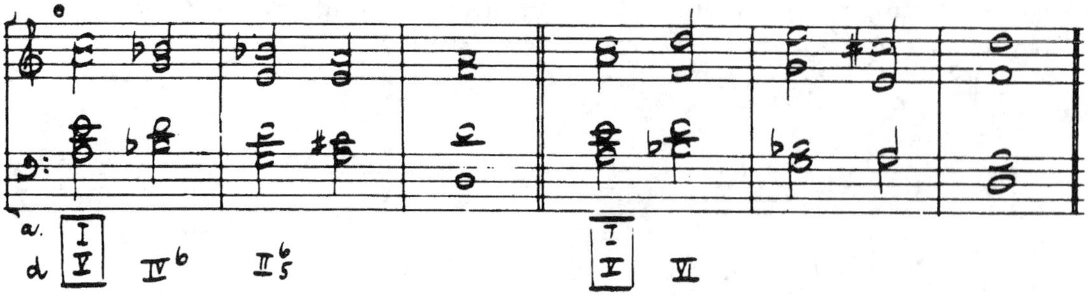

Modulations to the dominant, the subdominant, and the relative minor keys are to be found in practically every piece of music written during the so-called "classical" period; they are in fact fundamentals of musical construction. In order to extend them slightly and render the effect less abrupt, composers frequently pass through an intermediate key before reaching the ultimate destination. The possible combinations of this sort are almost infinite, but a few of the commonest are diagrammed below.

If the dominant key is the ultimate goal, the intermediate key may be either the relative minor of the tonic or the relative minor of the dominant; in other words, C - a - G, Ex. 9-a, or C - e - G, Ex. 9-b.

If the modulation is to the subdominant, the relative minor of either may serve as intermediate. C - a - F, Ex. 10-a, or C - d - F, Ex. 10-b.

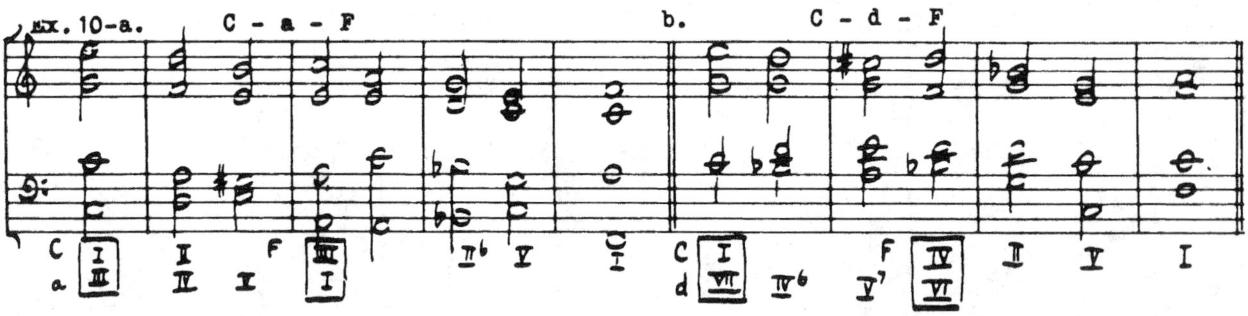

Two further illustrations are appended: from C major to A minor by way of F major, and from A minor to D minor by way of F.

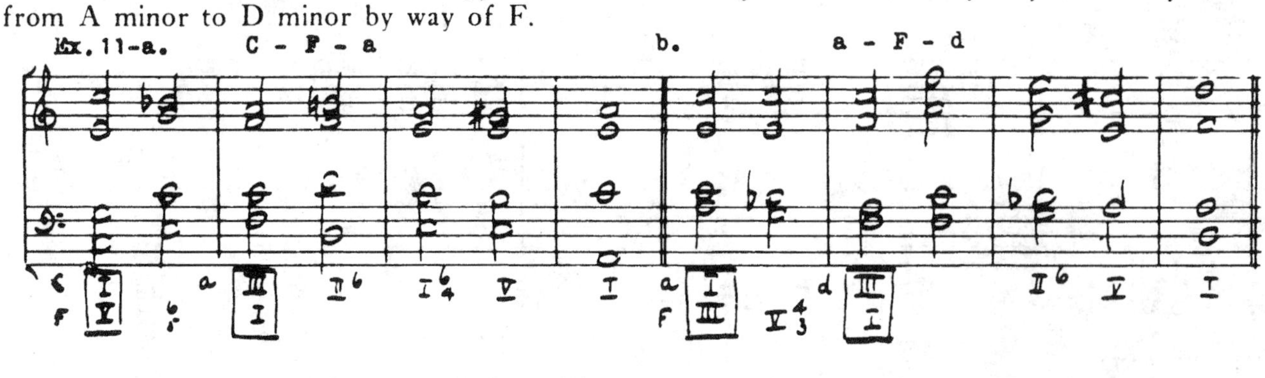

Since any complete musical composition must begin and end in the same key, it is obvious that if a modulation occurs in its course a retransition to the principal key must be effected. Such a modulatory "round-trip" is illustrated in Ex. 12. The student should construct for himself diagrams of similar modulations to and from all the related keys.

Ex. 12 a - C - a

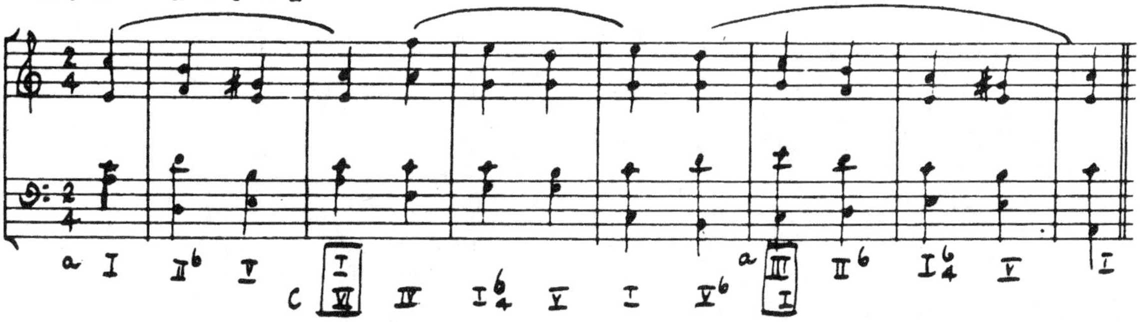

Exercises: The student should write, or better, *play* examples of all the modulations illustrated in this chapter, starting from various keys which may be assigned by the instructor. These should not be mere transpositions of the models, but should be carefully worked out individually.

Continue the following patterns as a series of *complete cadences* in the indicated keys. Indicate the common chord at each modulation; arrange the rhythm so that the new tonic always comes on the downbeat, if necessary repeating some of the chords with or without inversion, or adding others; all the rules of good part writing must be *strictly observed;* try to write a good melody.

1.

2.

3.

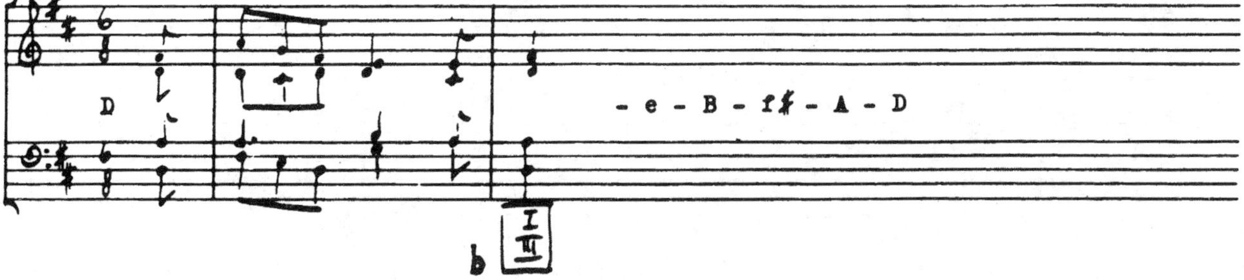

CHAPTER XIX

HARMONIZATION OF CHORALE MELODIES

The term "Chorale" is applied to the hymns of the Lutheran Church, many of which have been harmonized by J. S. Bach, although in most cases he did not compose the melodies themselves. The harmonization of these chorale melodies will give the student practice in simple modulation, as well as an opportunity to review the basic principles of four part writing as applied to more extended forms. The following illustrations should be carefully studied:

1. God of Heaven and Earth

2. What God does, that is well done

3. Jesus, my Joy

Phrase Structure. The chorale melody is divided into phrases which correspond to the lines of the text. Each phrase, the end of which is usually marked by a hold, concludes with a cadence either in the principal key or a related one.

The initial period. The first two lines of the text frequently express a complete thought, forming a sentence of two phrases with a comma at the end of the first and a period at the end of the second. This form is often reproduced in the music, where the first phrase ends in a semi-cadence, (the musical equivalent of a comma), or a full cadence in the *dominant key,* and the second phrase in a full cadence in the principal key, Ex. 1.

Sometimes the first phrase of a pair forming a period will conclude with a full cadence in the principal key, in which case it will usually be an "open" type, that is, with third or fifth in the melody, rather than a "closed" cadence, with root in soprano as well as bass, Ex. 2.

Occasionally the first period will consist of three phrases instead of two. In this case the last one will have a closed full cadence, and the other two may be open, semi- or dominant cadences, Ex. 3.

The intermediate phrases usually, though not always, cadence in related keys, for the sake of tonal variety. In Ex. 1 the third phrase cadences in the supertonic key; in Ex. 2, phrases three, four and five use the dominant, subdominant and again the dominant keys, and in Ex. 3 phrase four cadences in the relative major and phrase five in the dominant minor. The tendency is to *avoid keys used in the initial period.*

The final phrase will end with a complete cadence in the principal key, and may reproduce the melodic pattern of the ending of the initial period; in this case it may have a similar harmonization, though this is not obligatory, Ex. 1, 3.

2 **Cadences.** In *full cadences,* the note under the hold is usually the root of the concluding tonic triad, and clearly indicates the key to which a phrase has modulated. Occasionally the last note will be the third, rarely the fifth.

In the *semicadence* either the third or the fifth may occur as the last note; the root is extremely rare.

Often the same cadence melody may be harmonized in two or three different ways; it is important to consider all possible harmonizations, as one may be much more effective than the other. In doubtful cases a portion of the scale may be derived from the concluding notes of a phrase, which may then be tested for various possibilities.

4.

An extremely common cadence formula illustrated in Ex. 4 involves the use of devices which will be given detailed discussion in later chapters, but which are of such frequent occurrence in chorale harmonizations that they must be included here. The essential feature is the *dissonance of a second between keynote and supertonic,* occurring on the strong beat just before the final note of a phrase; this dissonance is resolved on the intervening weak beat, the voice having the keynote moving down to the leading tone. The result in Ex. 4-a is what is known as a *suspended leading tone* in the dominant chord, indicated by the figures $V_{4\ 3}$. Note that the keynote is present in the same voice in the preceding chord. An alternative treatment illustrated in example 4-b results in a six-five chord, usually described as supertonic, though in effect it is really a subdominant with added sixth. The important factor is the accented dissonance and its resolution; it is almost always used *whenever the supertonic note in the melody is repeated or prolonged through two beats just before the final note of the phrase.*

3 **Modulations.** The modulations of the various phrases are invariably effected through *common chords.* After deciding upon a modulation it is usually best to make it as early as possible in the phrase. *Between phrases there is no relaxation of the rules of good part-writing;* the only exceptions are an occasional chromatic change, or cross relation.

While a dominant seventh chord may sometimes be sufficient to suggest a modulation, as a rule a complete cadence is necessary: that is, some form of subdominant or supertonic of the new key must be used before the dominant and tonic chords. Remember that the key signature of the principal key is always in force; wherever, in the course of a modulation, it does not form part of the new scale, its effect must be cancelled by the use of the proper accidentals.

The Bach chorale settings contain a large number of non-chord tones which will be discussed in a later chapter. The melodies given below contain no non-chord tones, and should be harmonized as simply as possible. *Suggested procedure: first,* determine the key in which each phrase terminates; *second,* work out the diaphony, supplying Roman letters and indicating inversions as well as possible alternate harmonizations; *third,* check to see that strong changes occur at strong rhythmic points, that harmonic syncopations are avoided, and that the bass part is vigorous and effective; *fourth,* fill in the inner parts; *fifth,* check the whole result, with particular care to *see that the correct accidentals have been supplied to indicate all modulations.*

CHORALES

1. Lord Jesus Christ

2. Lord, I have done amiss

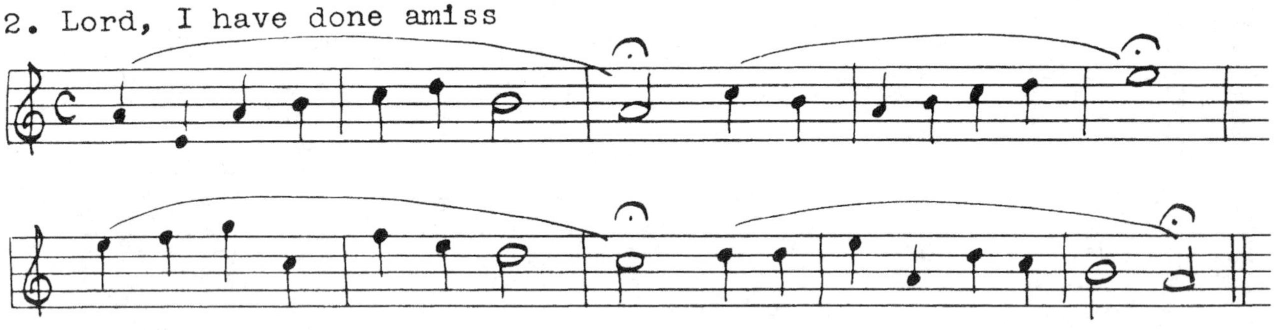

3. Strike me not in Thy wrath

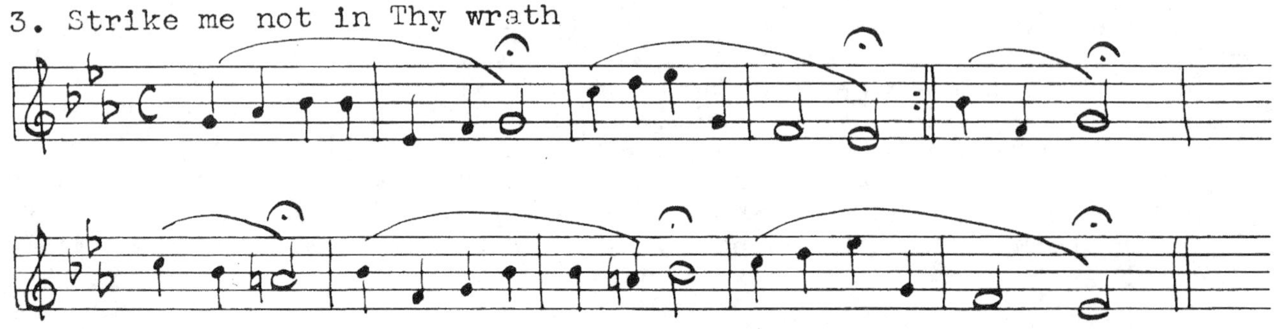

4. My inmost heart doth yearn

5. Eternity! Thou thunderword

6. O sadness

7. Praise to the Lord

8. How brightly shines the morning star

9. Christ lay in bonds of death

10. The day of days hath dawned

CHAPTER XX

CHROMATIC TRIADS

The alteration of one or more tones of a chord by accidentals not contained in the signature produces a *chromatic chord.* Such chords are useful to provide harmonic variety and color without causing changes of tonal center. The simpler chromatic chords may be divided into three groups: 1. chromatic triads, 2. chromatic seventh chords, and 3. augmented sixth chords.

In a sense all chords in the minor mode containing the raised sixth or seventh scale steps are chromatic chords, but as the purpose of these chromatic alterations is to confirm and reinforce the feeling of tonality, rather than to provide harmonic variety, they do not fall within the scope of the present chapter.

1 **Consonant chromatic triads** are either major or minor. Of these the most useful is the chromatic major triad, which is usually heard as a *dominant,* because among all the diatonic triads the dominant triad is the only one which is *always major under all circumstances.* (As we have seen in the chapter on the minor mode, a minor triad on the dominant tone does not function as a dominant chord, being useless for purposes of tonal definition.) These chromatic major triads produce the effect of authentic cadences in closely related or neighboring keys, and we may therefore call them *neighbor dominant triads.*

2 **Neighbor dominant triads** may precede any major or minor triad within a given key. The chord selected for this treatment is thought of as a temporary tonic, and the neighbor dominant triad is erected upon the tone a perfect fifth above (or perfect fourth below) its root, Ex. 1.

Ex. 1

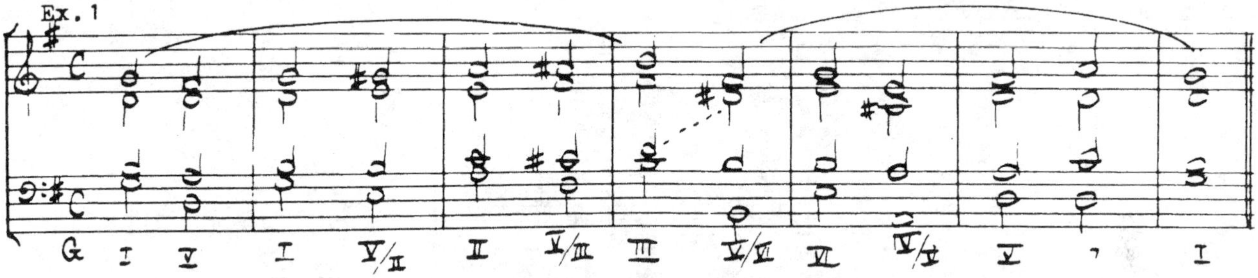

As these chords are to be thought of as dominants of the chords which follow them, and *not* as altered forms of diatonic triads, they should be indicated as V of the following chord; the diagonal line is a convenient substitute for the word "of".

Rhythmically these chords may be placed on either strong or weak beats; the color effect is obviously heightened by placing them upon accented beats. Observe the facility with which they harmonize ascending chromatic scales. Cross relations (Ex. 1, meas. 4) are sometimes unavoidable.

3 **In minor keys** any major or minor triad resulting from the use of either melodic or harmonic scales may be preceded by its own dominant, provided that good melodic voice leading results, Ex. 2.

Ex. 2

4 **The first inversion** of a neighbor dominant triad is frequently useful, and a more melodic bass is often attained in this way, Ex. 2 and 3.

5 **A deceptive progression** of a neighbor dominant triad sometimes occurs. In this case the chord in the principal key is thought of as *submediant;* if it is major, it will be preceded by a neighbor dominant on the semi-tone below; if minor, on the whole tone below, Ex. 4.

Ex. 3

Ex. 4

Note: The tonic six-four chord (deferred dominant) often intervenes between a neighbor dominant of V and the V chord itself, as in the above example.

6 **The "Neapolitan" chord** is a major triad on the lowered second scale-step, and unlike other chromatic major triads does not give the impression of being dominant in effect. The historical derivation of the term "Neapolitan" is obscure, but it makes a convenient label. It is most frequently used as a first inversion, ("Neapolitan Sixth") and undoubtedly evolved historically as a result of a chromatic alteration of the second scale-step in the melody of the familiar cadence formula: II_6 - I^6_4 - V - I in minor keys. Its usual progression is into the tonic six-four, or directly into some form of dominant harmony, Ex. 5.

Ex. 5.

The Neapolitan chord may also be used in both root position and second inversion, and frequently occurs in major keys, where it is necessary to chromatically lower its *fifth* as well as its root, Ex. 6.

Ex. 6

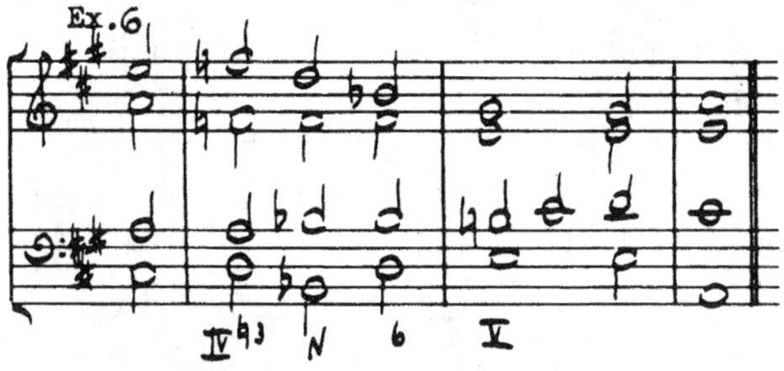

In resolving the root position directly to V, the resultant tritone in the bass is sometimes used, Ex. 7-a. The augmented second in Ex. 7-b, however, should be avoided by doubling the third of the Neapolitan chord. The various positions of this chord may be used in any desired succession, as long as the last one resolves correctly. The N^6_4 may proceed directly into V, Ex. 7-c, or into I^6_4 *in minor keys only,* Ex. 7-d. Notice that in both cases it is necessary to double the *root* and not the fifth of N^6_4

7 **Chromatic minor triads,** as well as major, are often borrowed from the minor key having the same keytone; the result is a certain ambiguity of mode, Ex. 8. The reverse process, that is, borrowing from major into minor, tends to obliterate the feeling of the minor mode, and is therefore of little value.

8 **Dissonant Chromatic Triads.** These are of two types, the augmented triad, with major third and augmented fifth, and the diminished triad, with minor third and diminished fifth. Any other chromatic combinations, such as minor third and augmented fifth, produce chords indistinguishable in sound from those already discussed.

An augmented triad may be formed from any major triad by raising its fifth a semitone. The augmented tonic and dominant triads are the most useful, Ex. 9.

If the chord is in fundamental position the augmented fifth is most satisfactorily resolved to the chord whose root is a fourth above. If this procedure is applied to the IV in major or the VI in minor keys, the resolution is outside the key, Ex. 10-a. Note, however, the Neapolitan chord which results in Ex. 10-b.

Note: Observe that

1. a chromatically altered tone normally proceeds *stepwise in the direction of its alteration;*

2. if the chromatically altered tone produces a dissonance, it is seldom doubled; observe the unusual doubling which results in Ex. 9, measure 5.

A diminished triad may be derived from any minor triad by lowering its fifth a semitone. Since diminished triads are little used in fundamental position, these chromatic chords almost invariably appear in their first inversions. The resulting chords will function either as supertonic sixths, Ex. 11-a, b, or as leading tone sixths, Ex. 11-c, d, e. The latter, which are in effect incomplete dominant sevenths, give the effect of *neighbor dominants.*

Note that in Ex. 11-d the chromatic tone is doubled; the active dissonance in this chord is the *leading tone,* (in this case C,) the doubling of which should therefore be avoided, rather than the G flat. In chromatic writing, problems of doubling are usually settled on a melodic basis, using a distribution which provides the most favorable possibilities of resolution.

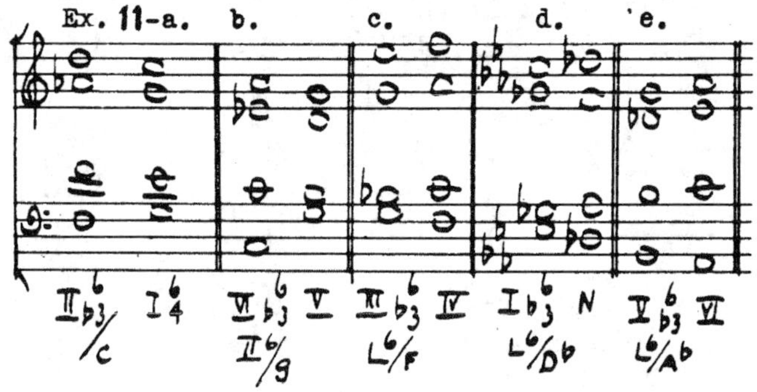

Exercises; the sign * indicates chromatic triad or its inversion.

4.

5.

6.

7.

8.

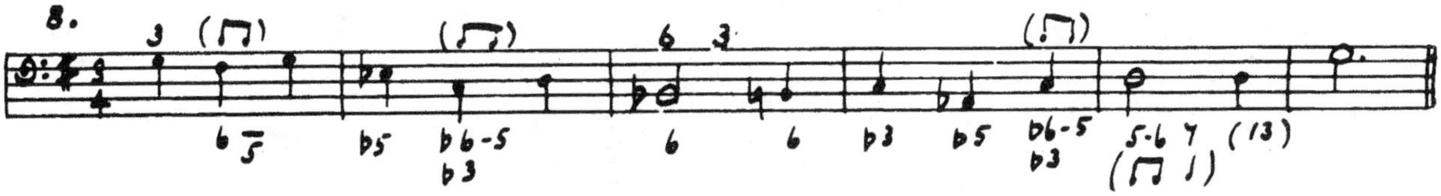

9.

10.

CHAPTER XXI

NEIGHBOR DOMINANT SEVENTH CHORDS

1 **Formation.** The addition of a minor seventh to any neighbor dominant triad produces a chord of the dominant seventh type which is one of the most useful of all embellishing chords. The neighbor dominant seventh chord is sometimes used in fundamental position, but since one of the chief functions of the seventh is to produce smoother and more melodic voice leading, the chord is more often used in inverted form, Ex. 1.

Ex. 1

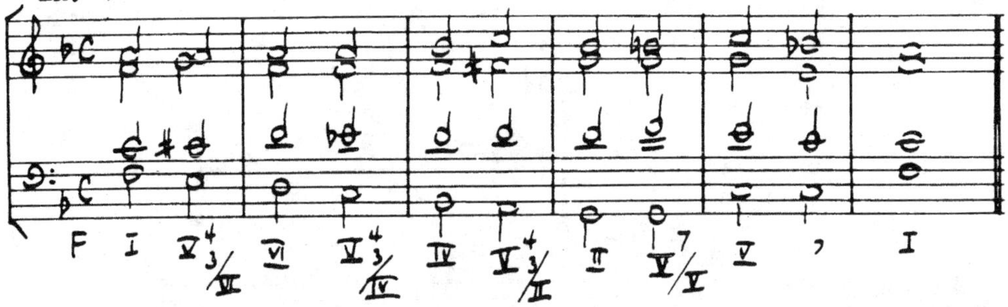

2 **Use of accidentals.** Observe that the necessary accidentals must always be used to make this chord a true *dominant seventh type,* — that is: root, *major* third, perfect fifth and minor seventh. Thus to form the neighbor dominant seventh of III in C major, *two* accidentals are necessary, D# and F#; chord: B, D#, F#, A. After the notes of the chord have been found, *select the bass note first,* choosing the one which is nearest to both the preceding and following bass notes. It may be the same as the preceding note, Ex. 2-a; it may be a chromatic passing tone, Ex. 2-b, or a diatonic passing tone, Ex. 2-c; it may be approached by a leap of a third, Ex. 2-d, or the *downward* leap of a diminished fourth, Ex. 2-e; wider leaps should be avoided. It may never be *left by a leap,* unless the chord is in root position, Ex. 2-f. After the bass note has been selected the positions of the other notes are easily determined, keeping in mind the general rules of good voice leading.

Ex. 2-a. b. c. d. e. f.

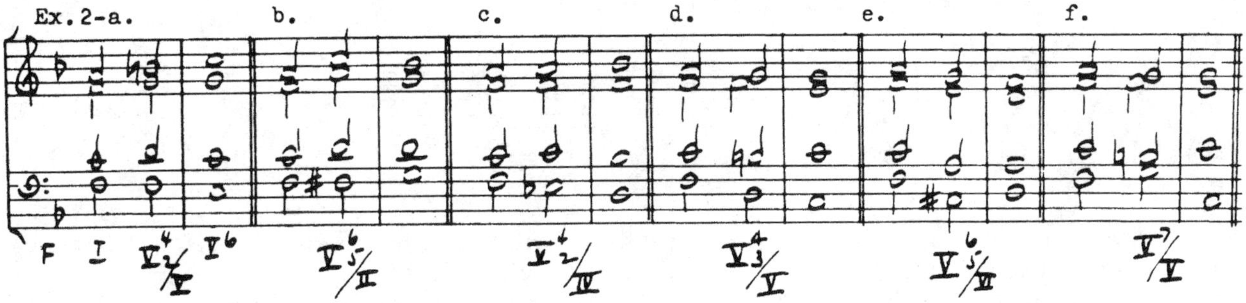

The tonic six-four chord often intervenes between the neighbor dominant seventh of V and its resolution, Ex. 3-a. If the neighbor dominant seventh resolves directly into V seven, Ex. 3-b, we have an example in the tenor part of "expedient false notation"; the correct melodic spelling of this part would be C, C flat, B flat, A, but as C flat is not a member of the neighbor dominant chord it is necessary to write it as B natural, although it continues downward.

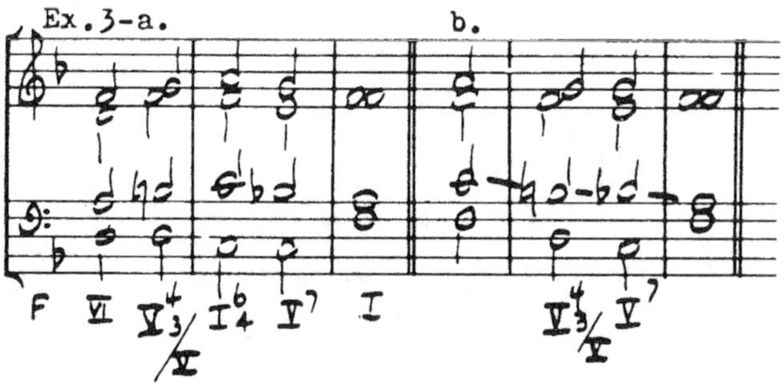

3 **Deceptive Resolution.** Some neighbor dominant sevenths may be resolved "deceptively." Recall (as stated in Chapter XX, Sec. 5) that a major triad must be preceded by a neighbor dominant on the semitone below, and a minor triad by one whose chord-root lies a whole tone below, in order to conform to the pattern of the deceptive resolution. Ex. 4 illustrates some of the more useful forms. As in the typical deceptive resolution, it is usually best and sometimes necessary in all these progressions to double the *third* of the chord of resolution.

* *Note*, Ex. 4-e, that the dominant seventh of the minor triad on the leading tone is available for this "deceptive" treatment. As it is not strictly a neighbor, it is best indicated by its key letter, in this case, b.

The Neapolitan sixth may be resolved into the neighbor dominant seventh of V, Ex. 5. The doubled root of the Neapolitan chord should be placed in the upper two voices.

4 **Signs.** In the following melodies, the location of some neighbor dominants is indicated by the sign *, others the student is expected to find for himself. In later chapters, where they are mixed with other chromatic chords, they are indicated by the sign ND . In analysis they should be indicated by the signs V_7/IV, V^4_3/II, etc. In some cases, such as those where "deceptive" resolutions occur, it may be helpful to substitute for the second Roman numeral the key letter from which the dominant seventh is borrowed: V^6_5/F, V^4_2/g, etc.

EXERCISES, with Neighbor Dominant Sevenths

CHAPTER XXII

NEIGHBOR DIMINISHED SEVENTH CHORDS

1 **Formation.** Any major or minor triad in a given key may be preceded by a diminished seventh chord based upon the semitone below its root; this semitonal neighbor thus functions momentarily as a leading tone, Ex. 1.

Ex. 1.

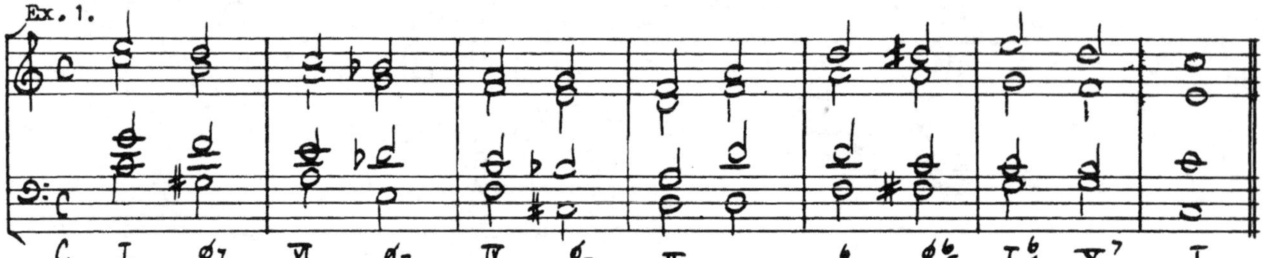

As diminished seventh chords are really incomplete dominant ninth chords, this is merely an extension of the neighbor dominant principle, Ex. 2, and such chords may be termed *Neighbor Diminished Seventh Chords.*

Ex. 2-a. b. c. d. e.

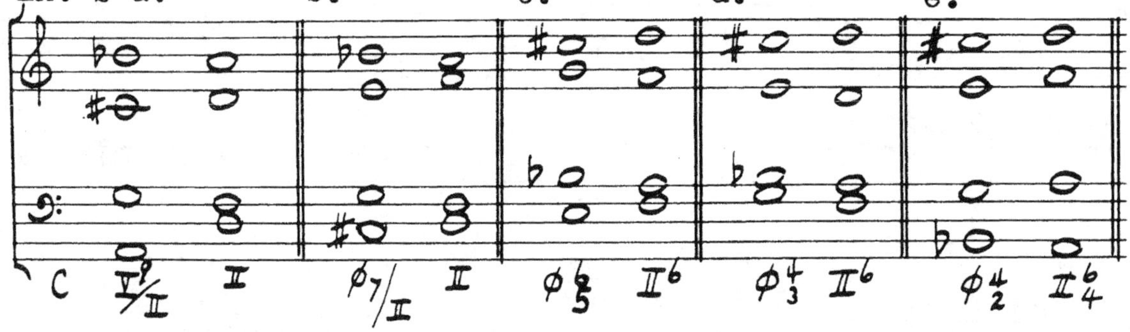

If the chord of resolution is in its first inversion, the neighbor diminished seventh may be used in either first or second inversion, Ex. 2-c, d. The third inversion, resolving into a six-four, is of limited usefulness, Ex. 2-e.

These chords may be approached by the leap of an augmented second, provided that it is in an inner part, Ex. 1, meas. 2. Parallel fifths in their resolution must be carefully avoided, however, even if the result is a doubled major third in the chord of resolution.

2 **Diminished seventh on the raised fourth degree.** In measure 5 of Ex. 1 we find a diminished six-five apparently based on D#, the leading tone of E minor (III), resolving to I^6_4. This is in reality a *passing chord,* both of the altered tones being chromatic passing tones, which is of such common occurrence in cadences that we may call it the diminished seventh on the raised fourth degree. It has two alternative spellings; Beethoven, in common with many composers of his era, usually spelled the chord as if it were the neighbor diminished seventh of V, Ex. 3; but in view of the chromatic complexity of modern music it is better to spell the chords, as far as possible, in conformity with their natural resolution tendencies, Ex. 4.

Ex. 3.
Beethoven: Sonata Op. 14 No. 2.

Ex. 4-a. b.

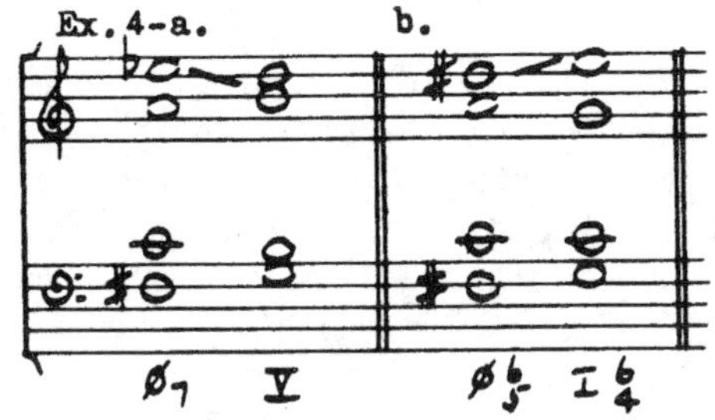

The two diminished seventh chords in Ex. 4 are identical in sound, but differently spelled because of the difference in their function. The function or purpose of E flat is to embellish D; the function of D sharp is to embellish E. Similarly the function of the first diminished seventh chord is to embellish the dominant chord; of the second, the tonic six-four. This emphasis upon the *function* of these chords brings out an important point with regard to chromatic chords and enharmonism in general: their use is explained not by what they *are* but by what they *do.*

Since the two chords in Ex. 4 are identical in sound, it is of no practical importance that one is based on F sharp, and the other, D sharp. They may be considered as groups of neighbor tones (except for common tones) of the tones of the chord of resolution; when placed as close together as possible above the bass tone they form *in sound* a group of three superimposed minor thirds; unless the resultant chord happens to be in fundamental position, one of these thirds will be spelled as an augmented second.

The diminished seventh chord on the raised fourth degree is frequently used as an embellishing chord between the Neapolitan sixth and the dominant or tonic six-four chords, Ex. 5. It is best to double the third of N_6. The effect is good in either mode; in resolving to the *major* six-four chord care must be taken to spell the diminished seventh chord correctly, Ex. 5-b.

Ex. 5-a. b.

3 **Other uses.** Every major triad has two embellishing diminished sevenths, a semitone apart in sound; one based upon the semitone below its root, and another whose seventh is a common tone with the root of the triad, Ex. 6. This latter chord, in its six-five position before the tonic, is identical with the chord on the raised fourth discussed in section 2 above. It is also available in root position, and any inversion. While possible before minor triads, the two common tones render it much less effective, Ex. 6-d.

Ex. 6-a. b. c. d.

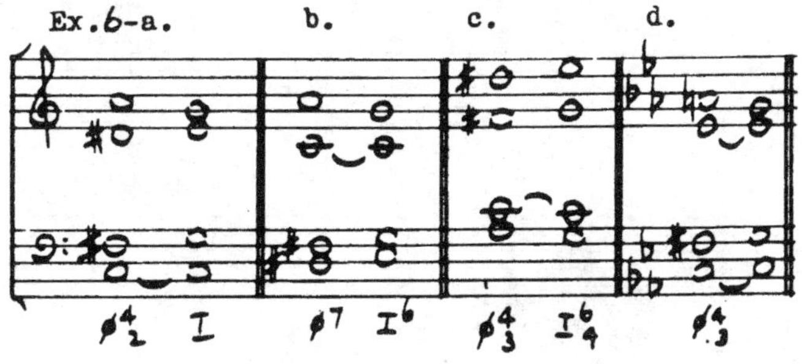

A diminished seventh chord is often inserted between V^4_3 and I_6 in the reversible progression illustrated in Ex. 7. It is really the result of one diatonic and two chromatic passing tones, as the crossing of the inner parts in Ex. 7-b makes clear. Probably because of its similarity to the neighbor dominant seventh of V, the diminished seventh chord in this latter example is usually spelled with F sharp in the soprano, rather than the more logical G flat.

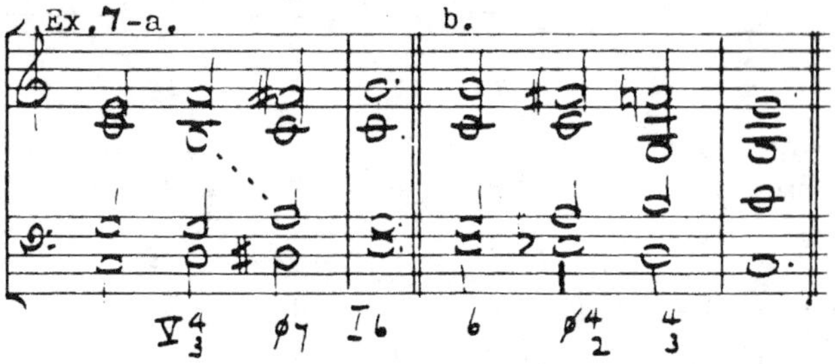

4 **Signs.** The signs $ø_7$, $ø^6_5$ etc. are used to indicate these chords, the figuring being derived from the position in the chord of the leading tone; as a matter of convenience the diminished seventh chord on the leading tone of the key (which is therefore not a neighbor) is indicated in the same manner. At times it may be helpful to indicate the leading tone upon which the chord is based, using a horizontal line as the abbreviation of the word "on". Thus the diminished seventh on F# may be indicated: $\frac{ø_7}{F\#}$

EXERCISES, with Neighbor Diminished Sevenths

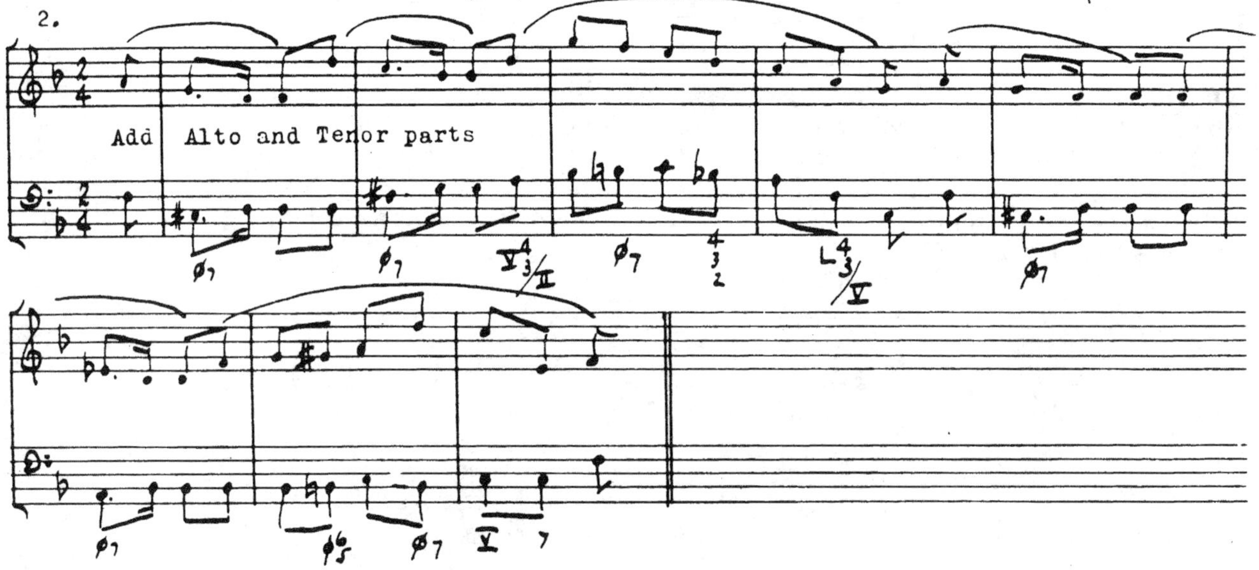

3.
4.
5.
6.
7.

CHAPTER XXIII

AUGMENTED SIXTH CHORDS

1 **Formation.** Many chromatic chords are the incidental product of various combinations of chromatic neighbor tones. In minor keys, the raised fourth scale-step sounded above the minor sixth scale-step produces the interval of an augmented sixth which characterizes an important series of chromatic chords known as augmented sixth chords.

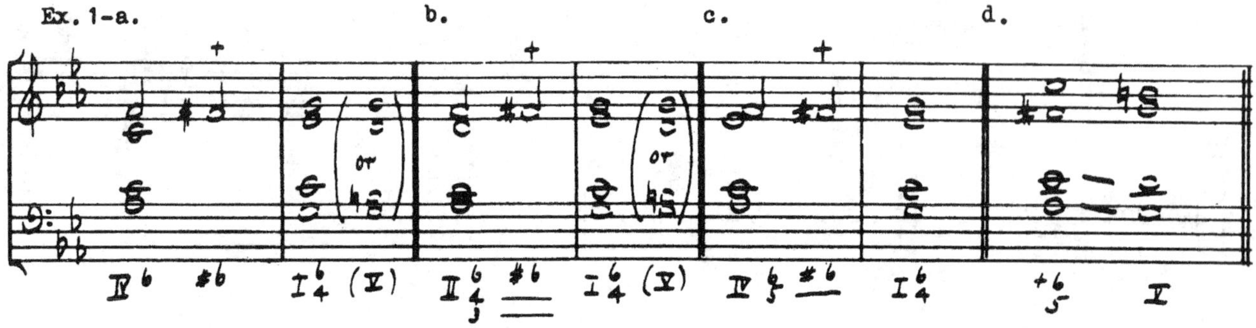

The first of these, sometimes known as the "Italian Sixth," consists of a bass tone, doubled major third and augmented sixth, Ex. 1-a. The second, the so-called "French Sixth," contains a major third, an augmented fourth and an augmented sixth above the bass, Ex. 1-b. The third consists of bass tone, major third, perfect fifth and augmented sixth, and has been called the "German Sixth," Ex. 1-c. It will be observed that, basically, all these chords consist of bass tone, major third and augmented sixth, and that the only variable tone is the fourth one, which may double (either at the unison or the octave) the major third, or add to the invariable chord members either an augmented fourth or a perfect fifth above the bass.

2 **Resolution.** As these chords are all altered forms of IV or II, the normal chords of resolution are I six-four and V. The resolution of the augmented six-five into V results in a type of parallel fifths which are often found, especially in the works of Mozart; these *semitonal* parallel fifths are often of good effect, especially when they are between the two-lower parts, Ex. 1-d; the student however, should use them sparingly.

3 **Chords without roots.** These passing or embellishing chords, containing from one to three chromatic neighbor tones of the chord to which they resolve, are entirely dependent for their form and arrangement upon the latter. The chord roots, two of which are chromatically altered, are of no significance (except to find the figuring) nor is there any purpose in indicating them with Roman numerals. The student should concentrate his entire attention on the *melodic movement* of each part, noting especially that *the augmented sixth will resolve by semitonal expansion,* either to the doubled fifth of I six-four or to the doubled root of V. Obviously the three upper parts may be rearranged in any desired manner, without affecting the form of the chord or its resolution, Ex. 2.

4 **Use in major keys.** In major keys it is necessary to lower the bass a semitone in order to form these chords. They may, therefore, be thought of as the result of *the simultaneous progression by contrary motion of the raised fourth and lowered sixth scale-steps.* While they are sometimes transposed to other degrees of the scale, the typical augmented sixth chord is always based upon the *minor sixth scale-step,* resolving to I $^{6}_{4}$ or V. Ex. 3-a.

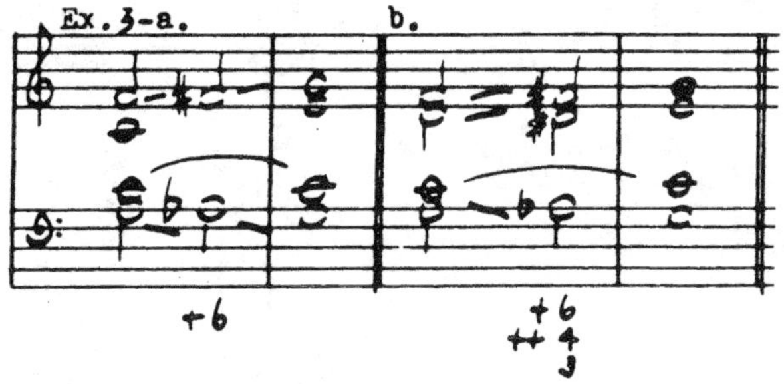

In major keys the resolution of the augmented six-five chord involves the upward resolution of the lowered fifth. This faulty spelling may be corrected by substituting the enharmonic tone for the lowered fifth, resulting in a *doubly augmented fourth,* Ex. 3-b. The term "doubly augmented sixth chord," sometimes used, is a misnomer, as it is the fourth that is doubly augmented. If the student will think of this chord as consisting, aside from the common tone, of three chromatic neighbors of I six-four, its structure and function will at once be apparent.

5 **Other Forms.** While the chords described above form the great bulk of those to be met with in the course of ordinary analysis, it is possible to rearrange the tones of these chords so that any of the other three tones, aside from the minor sixth scale-step, may appear in the bass. The figuring presents a somewhat complex picture; the simplicity of the actual procedure will be apparent if the student will merely remember that we are rearranging, in *vertical* order, three invariable tones, (in C major or minor: A flat, C, F sharp), and two variable ones, D, and E flat, together with the *enharmonic* of the latter, D sharp. If the raised fourth scale-step retains its position above the minor sixth, these chords may still be referred to as augmented sixth chords, although the latter interval does not appear in the figuring. Ex. 4.

6 **Diminished third chords.** If the relative positions of the raised fourth and minor sixth scale-steps are exchanged, the augmented sixth becomes by inversion a diminished third, and all of these chords may be referred to as *diminished third chords,* irrespective of their figuring, Ex. 5.

7 **Further Uses.** The diminished third chord on the raised fourth degree differs only by a semitone from the neighbor diminished seventh chord on the same scale step, and may be substituted for the latter before I six-four in the cadence, Ex. 6.

Augmented sixth and diminished third chords may often be substituted for neighbor dominant or diminished seventh chords. Thus the "French" sixth differs only by a semitone from the dominant four-three, and may, therefore, replace the latter chord before any major or minor triad in fundamental position, Ex. 7. When it occurs before the dominant chord, as in Ex. 7-a, the seventh is frequently added to the latter chord, in which case the augmented sixth (F sharp in the example) falls a semitone to the seventh (F natural) of V.

The diminished third chord derived from the "German" sixth differs only by a semitone from the neighbor diminished seventh, and may precede any major or minor triad in fundamental position, Ex. 8.

Any *major* triad in a given key may be preceded by an augmented sixth chord whose bass note lies a *perfect fourth* above, Ex. 9. These chords are equally effective with major or minor third, the latter often occurring as a chromatic passing tone.

Ex. 10 shows two common augmented sixth chords replacing the V^4_3 in the cadence. The parallel fifths in Ex. 10-b, as noted above, are considered good, particularly in instrumental writing.

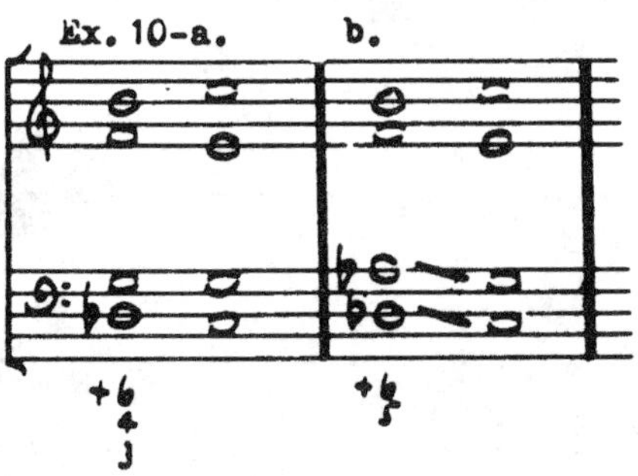

EXERCISES, GROUP I. Augmented Sixths

GROUP II. Augmented Sixths and Diminished Thirds

Add inner parts to each of the following:

6.

7.

8.

CHAPTER XXIV

NON-CHORD TONES

The texture of nearly all music contains a certain number of tones which do not belong to the basic chord structure, and which are therefore called non-harmonic or non-chord tones. Except for the so-called "free" tones, they are all neighbor tones, that is, they are not more than a whole step from the nearest chord tones which they precede or follow. Those that are unaccented contribute to a flowing style, filling up the intervals between chord tones, while those at accented points are strongly active, adding color and intensity to the effect.

1 **Passing and Returning Tones.** The most common types of unaccented neighbor tones are known as passing and returning tones. A *passing tone* is a non-chord tone introduced scalewise in passing from one chord tone to another. Thus between the root and third, or the third and fifth of any chord a single diatonic passing tone is available. Between the fifth and the root above it two diatonic passing tones may occur, provided that they are always used together. Chromatic passing tones are also available, singly or in combination; no passing tone may be approached or left by an interval greater than one whole step.

A *returning tone,* (also called embellishment, auxiliary or alternating tone), is a neighbor tone introduced between a chord tone and its repetition. Where the upper neighbor is used it is normally diatonic, but lower neighbors which are not already semitones are frequently chromatically raised. In the following illustrations the passing tones are indicated by the letter P, and the returning tones by R.

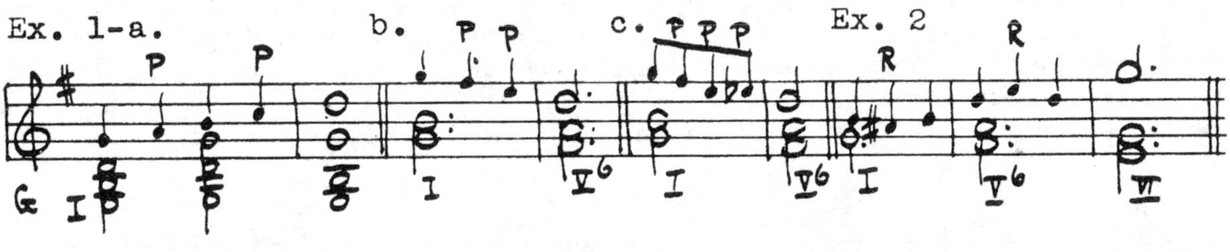

2 **Anticipations.** The only other unaccented neighbor tone approached and left stepwise is the *Anticipation,* (indicated by the letter A), which occurs most frequently in cadences. It is a tone sounded in advance of the other tones of the chord to which it belongs, making a discord against the harmony prevailing at the moment. It is nearly always of short duration, Ex. 3.

3 **Suspensions.** Accented neighbor tones are of two general types, those that are prepared, known as suspensions, and those that are not prepared. A *suspension* is produced by delaying the progression, between two successive chords, of any stepwise moving part, so that a tone held over from the first chord is heard as a discord against the remaining tones of the second chord. The delayed or suspended tone then enters, after the others, but usually before another chord change occurs.

A suspension thus involves three factors, the *preparation,* or tone in the first chord selected for prolongation, the *suspending discord,* or *suspension* proper, and the *resolution.* Rhythmically, the suspending discord always falls upon an accent, and may be indicated by the letter S.

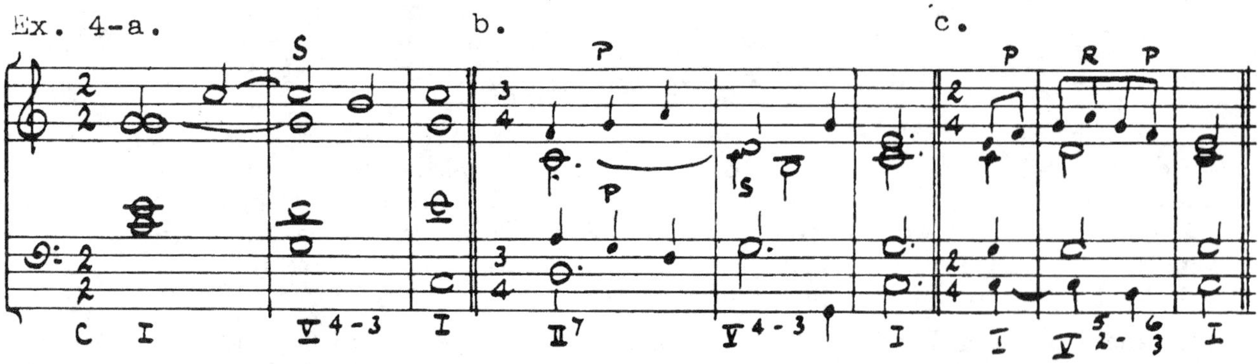

Ex. 4-a and b may be referred to as 4-3 suspensions, the figures indicating the respective distances from the bass of the suspending discord and its resolution. When the suspension occurs in the bass part, Ex. 4-c, the figures (2-3) refer to the intervals made by the suspension and its resolution with the chord tone *next* above it, the latter being determined by transposing the upper parts down into close position above the bass.

Ex. 4 illustrates a very common treatment of the cadence, already referred to in Chapter XIX, p. 81 , which may be called the *leading tone suspension.* It is made by sounding the keynote against some form of the *dominant* harmony. The suspending note, heard against the fifth of the dominant chord produces a seventh or second discord which provides the propulsive force in this very active progression.

The suspension 5-6 is possible in the bass, if the fifth be augmented, Ex. 5-a. The 7-6 suspension is perhaps the most frequent of all suspensions in upper voices, and may be freely used in sequence, provided the doubling part is carefully handled to avoid consecutives, Ex. 5-b. The delayed parallel fifths between soprano and alto in Ex. 5-c are considered good, but delayed octaves inadmissible. The 9-8 suspension in an upper voice is also available, Ex. 5-d.

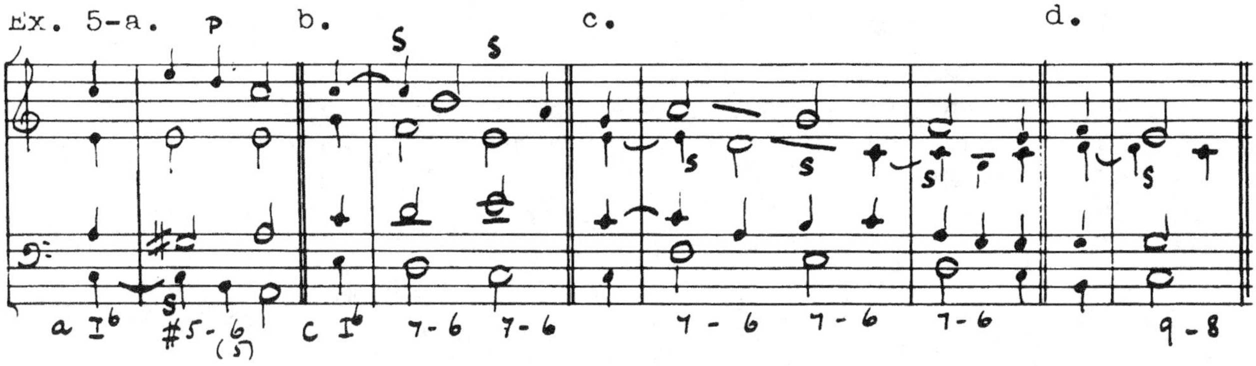

Note: The doubling should be carefully considered in the chord containing the discord of suspension. If the resolution note is a *major third,* and especially if it is a *leading tone, it should not be doubled.* Suspensions are always more effective if the resolution note is not sounded against the discord of suspension. However, there are a good many cases where this cannot be avoided, as in the 9-8 suspension.

As a rule the harmony does not change until after the suspension has resolved. However, it is possible to change at the moment of resolution to another chord, provided that this new chord also contains the resolution note, Ex. 6.

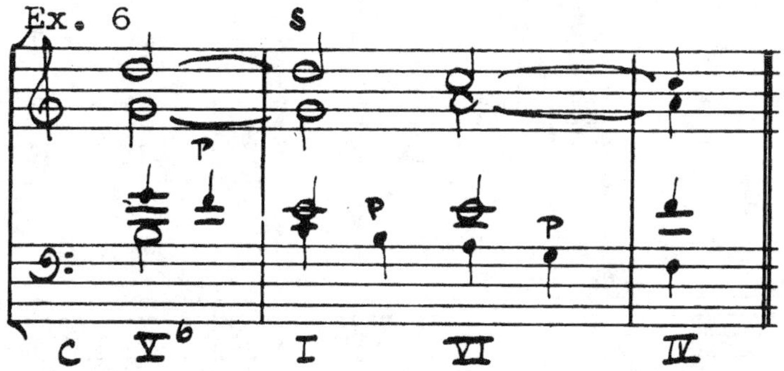

4 **Upward-resolving suspensions,** sometimes called *retardations,* though not used by sixteenth century composers, were gradually introduced by instrumental writers of later periods. The leading tone is often suspended in this way, and frequently the seventh of the dominant, when also present, is suspended at the same time, Ex. 7-a. Upward resolutions produce the numbers 7-8 and 2-3 in an upper voice, and 9-8 or 7-6 in the bass, Ex. 7-b, c, d.

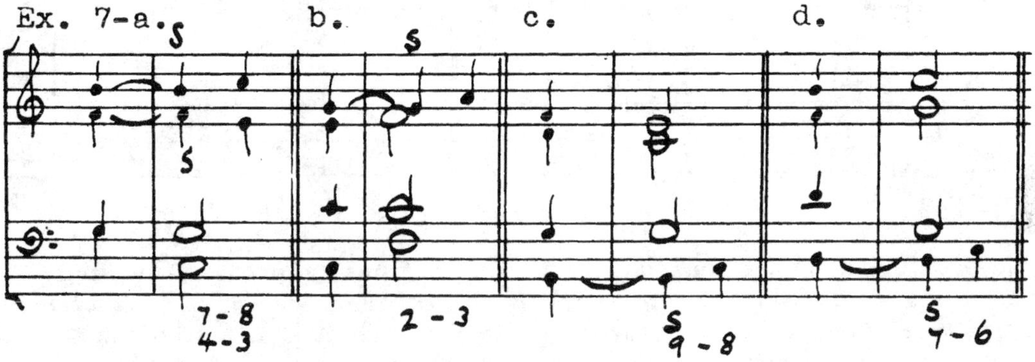

5 **Double suspensions** may occur when two parts move in parallel thirds or sixths, Ex. 8. The resolution of the tritone in Ex. 7-a is also a form of double suspension.

6 **Ornamental resolutions** are made by shortening the time value of the suspending discord and interpolating between it and the note of resolution one or more ornamental tones. For this purpose the other neighbor may be used, Ex. 9-a, or another note of the chord of resolution, Ex. 9-b, or various combinations of these with passing tones, Ex. 9-c. Ornamental resolutions are frequently applied to both parts of a double suspension, Ex. 9-d. If the lower neighbor, as ornamental note, is not a diatonic semitone, it may be chromatically raised.

Ex. 9-a. b.

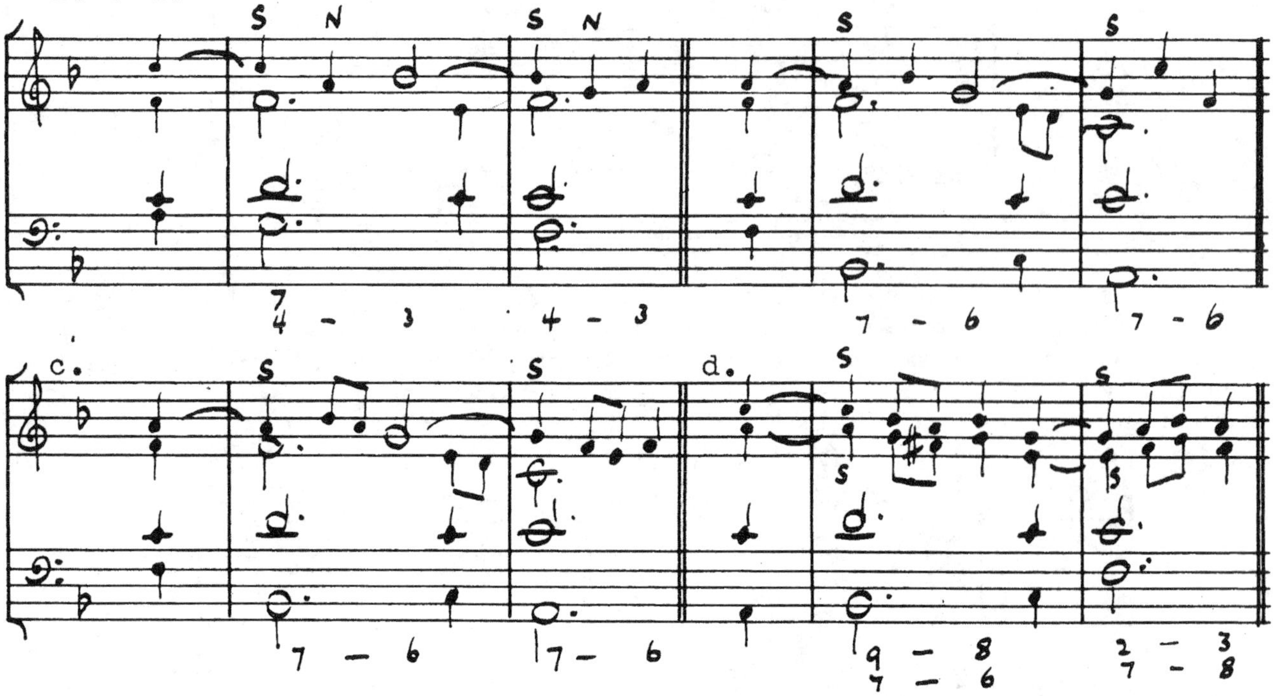

7 **Unprepared accented neighbor tones** are of two types, those approached by step, and those approached by leap. *Aside from the way in which they are approached, their treatment is identical with that of suspensions.* When approached by step, the effect is similar to that of the *changing note* (Nota Cambiata) of sixteenth century polyphony, a discord which changes place with a concord on the accent. To distinguish this type of neighbor tone from the others it may be indicated with the letter C, as in Ex. 10. Note that it may be immediately preceded by a passing tone or an anticipation of itself.

Ex. 10-a. b. c. d.

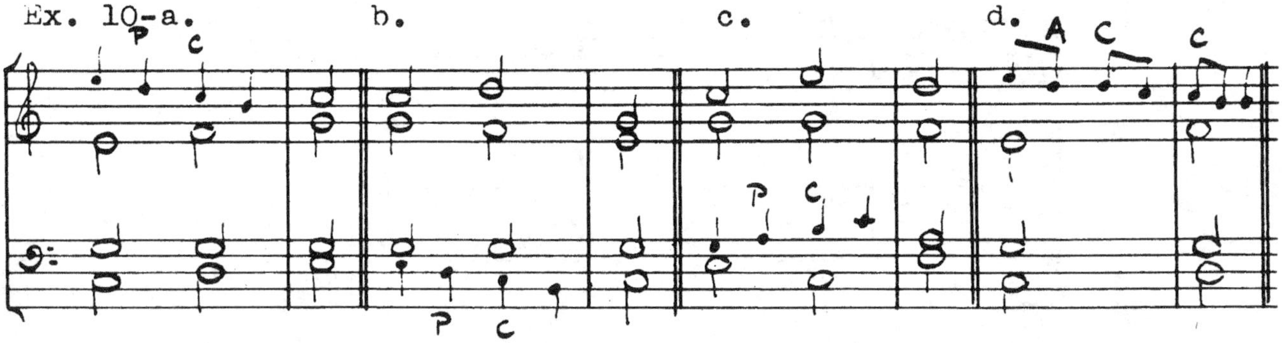

8 **Neighbor tones approached by a leap** are generally described as *appoggiaturas*. There seems no reason in an English text-book for perpetuating this clumsy and inconvenient word, which might better be translated as "leaning tone", and we will indicate them simply with the letter N, Ex. 11. Unprepared lower neighbors are much more common than upward resolving suspensions. "Leaning tones" are also used at weak rhythmic points, Ex. 11-c. and are very likely to be chromatic. They frequently occur in two voices at once, and may be anticipated on the preceding weak part of the beat, Ex. 12.

9 **Neighbor tones left by a leap** are rather rare; in most cases they belong to the following chord, and may therefore be called *free anticipations,* Ex. 13-a, though some do not fall in this category, Ex. 13-b. Occasionally a tone which is not a member of either chord may be found, approached and left by a leap. It is called a *free tone,* and indicated by the letter F, Ex. 13-c.

10 **Compound neighbor group.** An expressive device often used for ornamentation is the skip from one neighbor tone to the other before resolving to the principal tone. To avoid confusion with embellishing devices occurring simultaneously in two voices, such as double passing tones and suspensions, we will call this treatment a *compound neighbor group,* without regard for the way in which it is approached.

The historical antecedent of this device is the "changing note group" of sixteenth century counterpoint, which was invariably approached from above by step, and used first the upper and then the lower neighbor of the final tone, Ex. 14-a. Later instrumental writers have used the device with much greater freedom. It occurs as a compound returning tone group, Ex. 14-b, a compound passing tone group, Ex. 14-c, or a compound "leaning tone" group, Ex. 14-d. A great variety of rhythmic arrangements are possible, the strongest accent being frequently placed on one or the other of the two neighbors. The skip may be made in either direction; as a rule, the downward skip is approached from above, and the upward skip from below.

Ex. 14-a. b. c. d.

The following melodies, drawn from various sources, including the folk music of many nations, provide admirable material for the study of melodic ornamentation. The student is urged to attempt their immediate harmonization at the keyboard; remember that folk tunes utilize only the simplest chords; always maintain a steady rhythm, and the logic and expressiveness of the non-chord tones will at once be apparent.

FOLK TUNES

1. Lively English

2. Moderate Robin Adair Scotch

3. Well accented O Mary, don't you weep Negro Spiritual

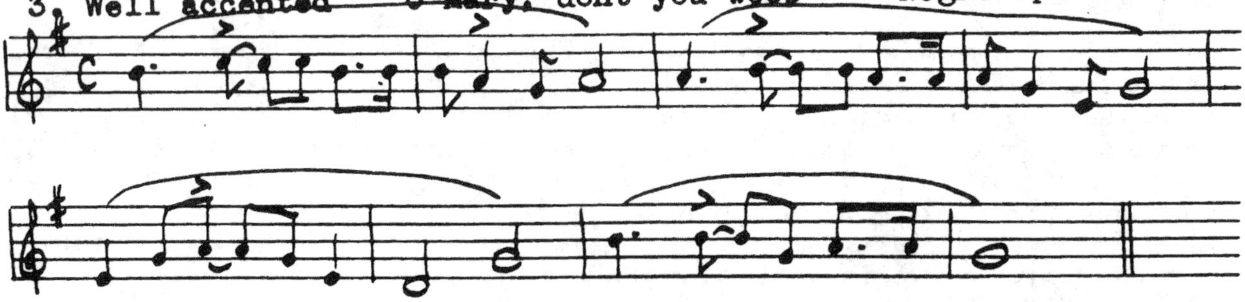

4. Fairly rapid — Leezie Lindsay — Scotch

5. Moderate — Christmas Song — German

6. Vigorous — When Johnny comes marching home — American

7. Flowing — French

8. Moderate Dutch

9. Slow My Lord, what a mourning Negro Spiritual

10. Moderate The Minstrel Boy Irish

11. Brisk The Arkansas Traveler American

12. Slow German

13. Moderate Gentle Annie Stephen Foster

14. Very slow Swedish

15. Swinging Italian

CHAPTER XXV

NON-CHORD TONES IN THE BACH CHORALE

1 Examination of the chorale settings by J. S. Bach reveals interesting aspects of his musical thought-processes. A strong feeling of melodic continuity is always apparent in every part; consequently neighbor tones taken by a leap are very rare, accented discords are either prepared or approached by step, and there is a very free use of passing tones. A statistical analysis presents certain difficulties because of the problem involved in determining which tones are to be considered "non-chord" tones. Because of their weak rhythmic location many tones may be considered passing tones which never-the-less form parts of incidental consonant chords. On the other hand, any tone which adds dissonance, such as a passing seventh, may be tabulated as "non-chord", though its rhythmic and melodic function is of far more importance than the question of whether or not it is foreign to the prevailing harmony.

Ex. 1 . Chorale: "Jesu, meiner Seelen Wonne"

Harm. by J. S. Bach

2 **Frequency Analysis.** An approximate tabulation of four well-known chorale harmonizations shows that passing tones predominate by more than four to one; in order of diminishing frequency of use the others are suspensions, changing tones, returning tones, anticipations, neighbor tones taken by leap. The student should add to the following table by making some further analysis of his own, and comparing the results with those given here.

Note: The numbers refer to the Breitkopf and Härtel collection known as the "371 Four-part Chorales".

	P	S	C	R	A	N
Ein' feste Burg, No. 273	58	6	4	1	0	0
Christ lag in Todesbanden, No. 8	23	14	2	1	0	0
Dies sind die heil'gen zehn Gebot', No. 127	20	4	2	1	0	0
Nun danket alle Gott, No. 32	17	4	0	2	4	1
	118	28	8	5	4	1

3 **Passing and returning tones.** *Passing tones* may be used singly, in pairs, (double passing tone) or in three parts at once. Double passing tones move either by contrary motion or in parallel thirds and sixths, Ex. 2. Triple passing tones may be written when a major or minor triad is followed or preceded by its own first inversion; two parts move in thirds, and the other by contrary motion; a doubled third always results, Ex. 3 and 4. *Returning tones* occur in a proportion of less than one in *twenty* passing tones. In imitating the Bach style, the student should exercise particular carė to avoid their excessive use.

4 **Suspensions.** The suspension most frequently used, as noted in the preceding chapter, is that of the leading tone in cadences. The active dissonance is produced by the clash of the prolonged keynote against the second scale-step, Ex. 5 and 6. Ornamental resolutions are frequent, employing passing tones or neighbor tones taken by a leap, Ex. 1, meas. 6 and 8; at times the chord changes as the suspension resolves, Ex. 7 and 8. Double suspensions are so rare that they cannot be considered as having any part in chorale style.

5 **Changing tones.** As defined in the previous chapter, the changing tone is a favorite device with Bach to draw attention to a melodic part. Aside from its very frequent use as a sort of accented passing tone, Ex. 9, it may be preceded by a passing tone, Ex. 10, or a returning tone, Ex. 11, and may occasionally be anticipated, Ex. 12. (The latter is also a favorite device of César Franck).

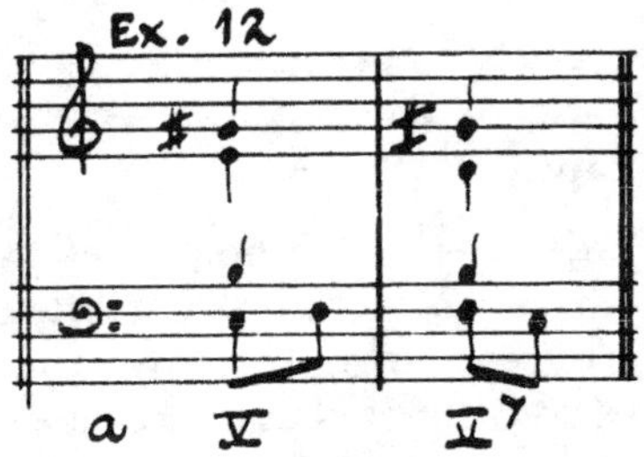

6 **Anticipations** are fairly common in cadences. They are sometimes double, moving in thirds or sixths, and an occasional free anticipation is found, Ex. 1 and 13.

7 **Neighbor tones** taken by a leap are confined almost entirely to the ornamental resolution of the suspension, Ex. 1, meas. 6 and 8. When left by a leap they are invariably free anticipations, Ex. 7 and 13.

8 Chromatic harmony. Bach produces some striking effects by the use of chromatic embellishing chords, including neighbor dominant and diminished sevenths, augmented sixths, diminished thirds, and the Neapolitan sixth. Although occasionally placed for emphasis in a strong rhythmic position, they are mostly the result of converging or diverging chromatic lines which include a number of chromatic passing tones, Ex. 14.

Ex.14 J. S. Bach: Chorale, "Wer nur den lieben Gott lässt walten"

9 Suggested procedure: Fill in the given Bach diaphonies, observing that the inner parts *avoid holding common tones,* but rather make free use of passing tones in contrary motion, often crossing each other, and making occasional octave leaps.

In harmonizing the chorale melodies for which no basses are given, first review Chapter XIX with care. Since the movement of the bass will often be correlated with that of the inner parts, it is probably best to try to think of a progression of three or four chords at a time, seeking for all possible ways of connecting them melodically through the use of the various devices enumerated above. Each problem may be considered separately and in turn from the standpoint of the possibilities for passing tones, changing tones and suspensions, and the best combination of all three selected.

The governing importance of the bass part must never be forgotten, and the distribution of melodic devices should be reasonably impartial among the lower three parts. Special vigilance is necessary to *avoid parallel fifths and octaves as a result of passing tones.* As a rule, the movement of all parts should cease under the hold.

NOTE: The ten chorale melodies given here continue the series begun in Chapter XIX, and are numbered serially so that a total of twenty are available for study and treatment in the various ways indicated. There is little value in merely copying the Bach originals, but *after* the student has done his best to produce a setting which conforms as closely as possible to the Bach style, it will be interesting and instructive to compare his results with the Bach settings. In order to facilitate this study a table is given below, in which, opposite the numbers used in this book, will be found the number of a setting in the well-known collection: "371 Four-part Chorales of J. S. Bach" published by Breitkopf and Härtel, and now available in an American reprint. Note particularly that this collection often contains several settings of the same melody (consult the index) which reveal highly interesting variants in the treatment.

Chorale No.	B & H No.
1	136
2	287
3	38
4	21
5	26
6	57
7	90
8	86
9	15
10	17
11	131
12	59
13	186
14	216
15	173
16	39
17	82
18	368
19	358
20	102

11. Dearest Jesus, we are here

12. Beloved Jesus, what is thy transgression?

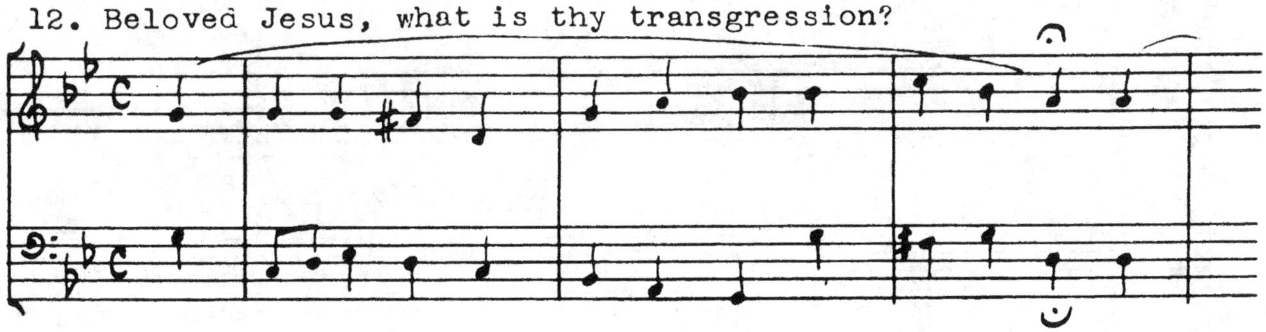

13. O God, hear my lament.

14. It is enough!

15. O heartfelt pain.

16. What shall I, a sinner, do?

17. O great and powerful God.

18. Help, Lord Jesus

19. My soul exalts the Lord.

20. Be of good cheer.

CHAPTER XXVI

MODULATION BY CHROMATIC CHORDS

1 **Remote Modulation.** Thus far we have discussed chromatic harmony with relation to a single tonality, and the only modulations met with were those of transitory character. From among the almost unlimited possibilities of modulation through chromatic chords we will select a few of the most useful for consideration. Many of these modulations involve enharmonic notation; and the keys attained are generally beyond the circle of related keys most easily reached by common chord modulation, (Chapter XVIII).

2 **Chromatic Triads.** While it is possible to connect *any* triad in a given key with *any* chromatic triad, bad consecutives usually result unless there is one common tone, and two of the parts move by contrary motion, Ex. 1-a. In Ex. 1-b there is no common tone. The effect of such progressions is nebulous, tonally speaking, and produces no special feeling of modulation.

3 **Triads and Chromatic Dominant Seventh Chords.** Any triad in a given key may be connected with any chromatic dominant seventh chord. These progressions are usually best when there is at least one common tone, Ex. 2-a and b, but may be managed without common tones, Ex. 2-c and d. Minor or even diminished triads are equally available as points of departure, and the chromatic seventh may follow either inversion, Ex. 2-e and f.

Exercise: Construct a table of dominant seventh chords which can be connected by a common tone with the C major triad, as begun in Ex. 3. Here the root of the triad is used successively as root, 3rd, 5th, and 7th of four different dominant seventh chords, the other parts proceeding to the nearest chord tones. The same process should be gone through with the 3rd and 5th of the triad.

4 **Successive Dominant Seventh Chords.** We have already encountered two dominant sevenths in succession in Chapter XXI, Sec. 2, Ex. 3-b. This pattern may be indefinitely extended, Ex. 4-a, and works equally well with inversions. The progression of a seventh chord or one of its inversions by *chromatic parallel motion,* Ex. 4-b, has been much abused, and is seldom of really artistic effect.

Ex. 4-a. b.

The connection of two dominant seventh chords having a common tone is readily understood from a study of the table given in Ex. 5, which shows all the dominant seventh chords which have a common tone with the C major V7. Starting with the root, each chord tone of the C major V7 is used successively as root, 3rd, 5th, or 7th of another V7. There are three sets of duplicates, Nos. 5 and 9, 6 and 11, 8 and 12. These are the smoothest in sound, and may be considered preferable to the others because each has two common tones and the remaining voices move *stepwise by contrary motion.* Of the others, those in which the parts move down (Nos. 1, 2, 3) are of better effect than those that move up (Nos. 4, 7, 10).

Ex. 5.

Exercise: Construct a similar table, using as the first chord an inversion of the V7 from some other key, and test the applicability of the above observation to your results.

5 **Incidental Modulation.** Any of these progressions may be employed as a means of modulation; many of them, however, sound very abrupt, and unless a sudden modulation is desired, much more artistic results can be obtained by a more gradual approach to the new key, especially if it is a remote one. It is often effective to pass through intervening keys, or to pass through the key which has one *more* sharp or flat in its signature than the objective key. Thus, E flat (three flats) is smoothly reached by passing through F minor (four flats), Ex. 6-a. In Ex. 6-b, the modulation from C to A is made by passing through E minor. Modulations to remote keys are usually facilitated by passing through related keys in the *opposite* mode, as illustrated in Ex. 6.

Ex. 6-a. b.

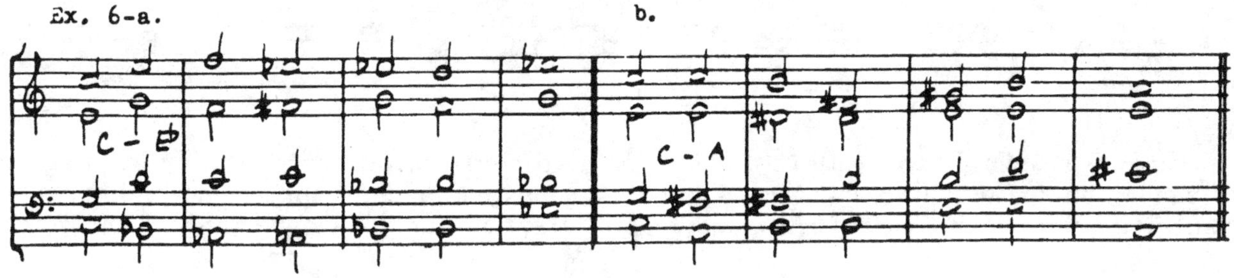

6 **Modulation through the Augmented Sixth Chords.** One of the most useful types of chromatic modulation is through the enharmonic transformation of any dominant seventh into an augmented sixth, resolving the latter interval by *semitonal expansion* into the six-four chord of the new key. It is not necessary to write the dominant seventh chord as an augmented sixth; the V_7 is merely resolved *as though it were an augmented sixth.* Ex. 7.

Ex. 7

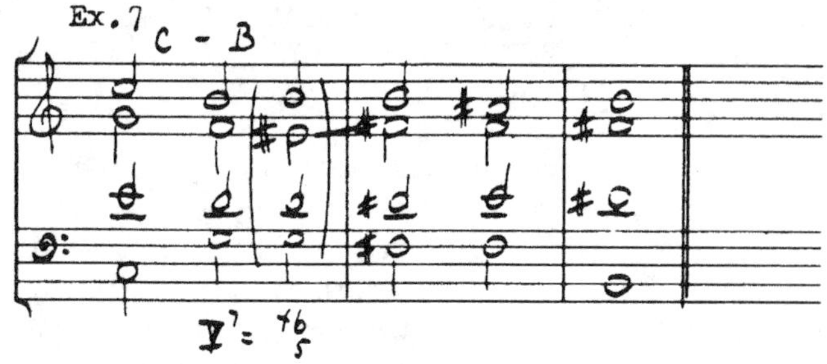

Dominant seventh chords formed upon the I, II, IV, and VI may also resolve in this way, Ex. 8. Those on III and VII, though possible, are less good. Excellent mental training is afforded by practising all these modulations at the keyboard.

Ex. 8—a.

7 **Modulation through the Diminished Seventh Chord.** The diminished seventh chord provides one of the simplest means of modulation to remote keys, but not always the best, as the resulting modulations are likely to be abrupt. As previously noted, the diminished seventh chord always sounds like a series of three superimposed minor thirds, no matter what the inversion or notation used. *In sound,* therefore, *there are only three diminished seventh chords.* Ex. 9.

Ex. 9.

The diminished seventh chord on D is identical in sound with the first inversion of the diminished seventh on B, and may be enharmonically spelled (like all the others) to represent a fundamental chord or any of the inversions. There are only two considerations to be kept in mind: correct spelling of the chord with regard to its resolution, and the avoidance of objectionable consecutives. A few of the many possibilities of resolution are illustrated in Ex. 10.

Ex. 10.

Since the diminished seventh chord contains no perfect octave or fifth it may be approached by similar motion of all voices, if necessary. In modulating, a diminished seventh chord may be constructed upon the semitone below the root of the tonic or dominant chord of the new key,

Ex. 11-a, b, c, and upon either the semitone below or the whole tone above the bass of the tonic six-four, Ex. 11-d and e. Spell these chords as simply as possible. Thus assuming the signature of C major, it is not necessary in Ex. 11-c to spell the tenor note of the diminished seventh chord B double flat, as would be the case in any key in which the A is flatted in the signature.

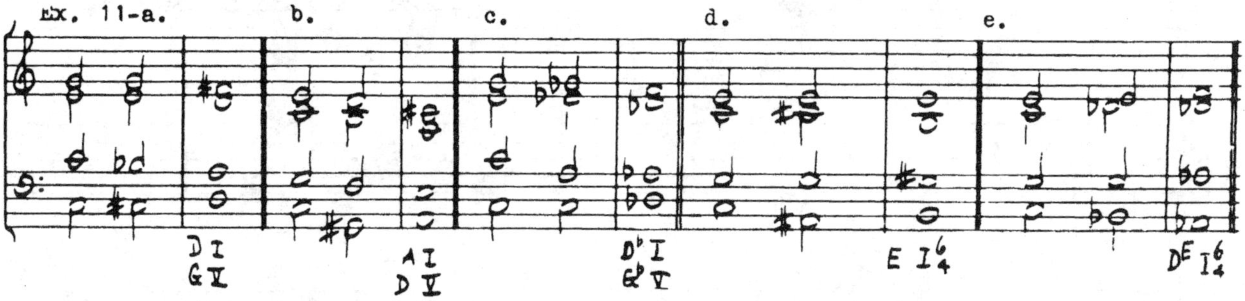

8 **Conversion.** It should be observed that any dominant seventh, fundamental or inverted, may be converted into a diminished seventh by raising its root, wherever found, a semitone. Similarly, a dominant seventh chord or inversion may be formed from any diminished seventh chord or inversion by lowering *any one* of the tones of the latter chord a semitone; the cadence will then follow in the key of the second chord.

Remember that the mere succession of V_7 and I in a given key does not establish that key; that a sequence of dominant or diminished sevenths tends to destroy all feeling of tonality, which must then be reestablished at the proper point by a complete cadence; and that it is always better to pass through an intervening key than to make a tastelessly abrupt modulation.

Exercises: a. Write, and if possible, play modulations from an assigned major key to all the unrelated major keys.

b. Do the same, alternately going from major to minor, and from minor to major.

c. Do the same, modulating from a given minor key to other unrelated minor keys.

d. Write several sentences of at least eight measures, using the beginnings given in Exercises 1 and 2, modulating to an unrelated key and then returning to the original key.

e. Add two inner voices to No. 3; in Nos. 4, 5 and 6, plan the modulations and write out the diaphony complete before attempting to fill in the inner voices.

EXERCISES, Remote Modulation

2.

3.

4.

5.

6.

CHAPTER XXVII

ALTERED CHORDS

1 The free application of chromaticism to any of the five main types of seventh chord described in Chapter XVII may easily obliterate their distinctive characteristics. Thus a dominant seventh becomes a minor seventh if its third is made minor. However, some chromatic variants are possible without confusing either type or function, and some are sufficiently frequent to merit description here.

2 **Altered major seventh chord.** A major seventh chord may have its fifth augmented; the major triad resulting between the upper three tones tends to sound dominant in effect and to establish the third of the chord as its real fundamental or root. The conflict between leading tones weakens the tonal function of the chord, the chromatic tone tending to dominate, Ex. 1.

The combination of a major seventh, augmented fifth and minor third produces a chord still more ambiguous, Ex. 2. The lower three tones form an enharmonic major first inversion, pointing up the enharmonic form of the augmented fifth as actual chord root, and relegating the seventh to the position of a neighbor tone.

3 **Altered Dominant Seventh Chord.** Chromatic alterations of the fifth of the dominant seventh chord are more useful. The augmented fifth tends to increase its resolution tendency, Ex. 3, although a doubled third will result in the chord of resolution. However its functional stability is impaired by the change, which introduces an augmented sixth with its divergent resolution tendency into the chord, Ex. 4 and 5.

The dominant seventh chord with diminished fifth is indistinguishable in sound from the augmented six-four-three, or "French" sixth, Ex. 6. In this case, however, the resolution tendency of the augmented sixth coincides with that of the leading tone, so that the tonal function of this chord is not weakened.

Ex. 1. 2. 3. 4. 5. 6.

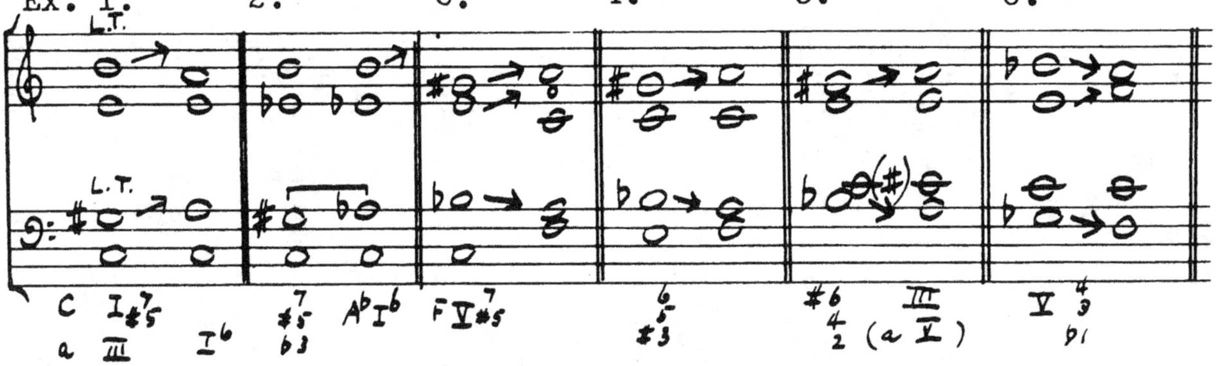

The remaining three types of seventh chord, minor, half-diminished and diminished, cannot be chromatically altered without losing their identity.

4 **Altered Dominant Ninth Chords.** Neighbor dominant ninth chords, or their incomplete forms (without root) may be erected upon the tonic, supertonic, mediant and submediant scale-steps. Of these the one on the supertonic is most useful, Ex. 7, because it resolves with equal facility into V or I^6_4 and its half-diminished form, Ex. 8, provides a useful embellishing chord on the raised fourth degree in cadences. Another derivative, Ex. 9, produces an augmented sixth chord of a type not previously discussed, in which both fifth and sixth are augmented.

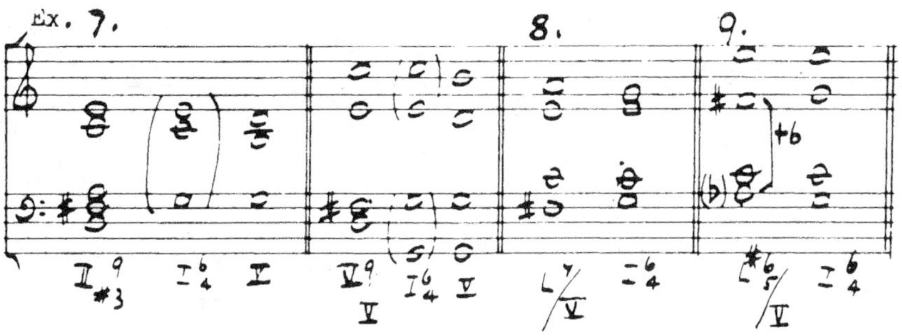

It should be observed that chromaticism of this type rather easily reaches a "saturation point", that is, a point beyond which the use of chromatics, instead of adding color, tends to cause many of the chords to resemble each other to a confusing degree. Furthermore, the addition of chromatic discords with conflicting resolution tendencies reduces and frequently cancels out the tonal function of a chord, resulting in a vagueness of direction which may lead towards "atonality", and can easily produce monotony.

EXERCISES Chromatic Seventh and Ninth Chords
Add Alto and Tenor parts to Nos. 1, 2, and 3

4.

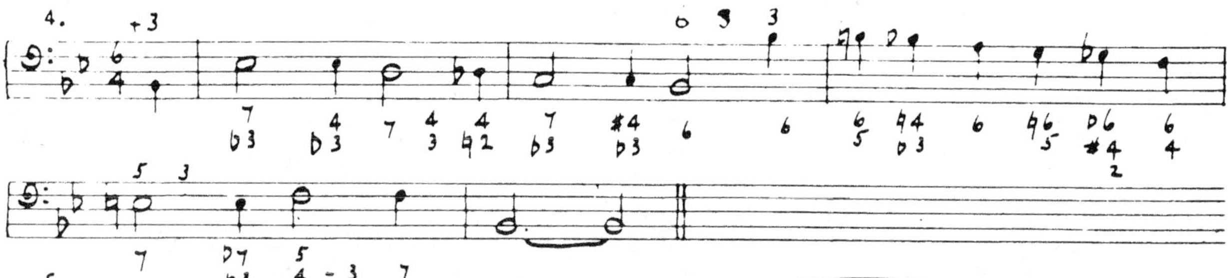

5.

CHAPTER XXVIII

MIXED CHORDS; THE PEDAL POINT

1 **Polyharmony.** The sounding of two or more different chords simultaneously produces an effect sometimes known as polyharmony. This device has been extensively used by modern composers, but its usefulness is limited by the difficulty of keeping the two or more chords from blending into a single harmonic unit. It was not by any means invented in the twentieth century, for any diatonic seventh chord is in effect a combination of two triads whose roots are a third apart, and ninth chords may be considered a combination of two seventh chords-similarly arranged so that all but two of their tones coincide.

2 **Mixed Chords.** More useful results are obtained from a mixture of chord and neighbor tones sounded together so as to emphasize the dissonance. The possibilities are large, but one type is so common, in "classical" as well as modern music, that it deserves special consideration. It consists of a group of three or more neighbor tones sounded above the root (or bass tone) of its normal chord of resolution. From the standpoint of evolution its original form was probably a triple suspension, such as Ex. 1-a and b, from which the chord of preparation was later omitted, Ex. 1-c. As a matter of convenience we will apply the term *mixed chords* to all such combinations.

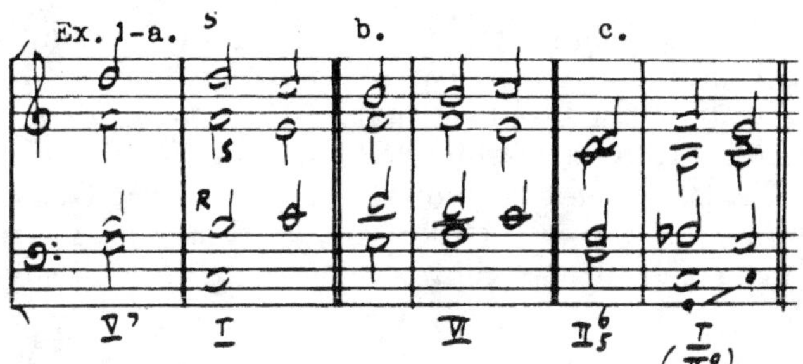

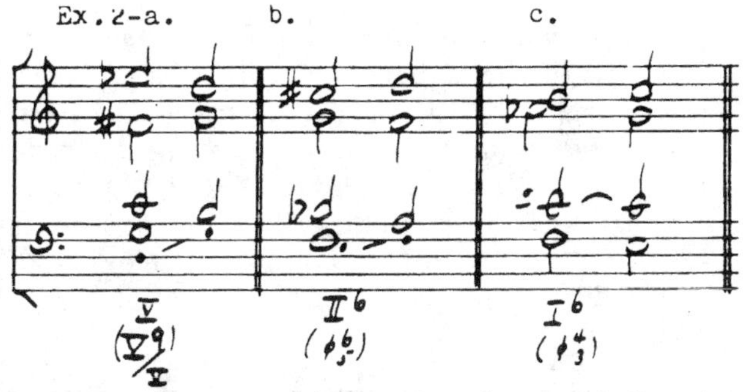

3 **Derivation.** This treatment may be applied to all neighbor dominant and diminished seventh chords, ninth chords and to most of the augmented sixth chords already discussed. In each case, a tone of the chord of resolution replaces one tone of the embellishing chord, and the three neighbor tones must form a recognizable part of one of the chromatic chords previously studied. Any major or minor root triad or first inversion may serve as chord of resolution.

Ex. 1-c and 2-a illustrate such chords formed from minor ninths resolving to major root triads. In Ex. 2-b and c the mixed chords are derived from diminished seventh chords resolving to first inversions.

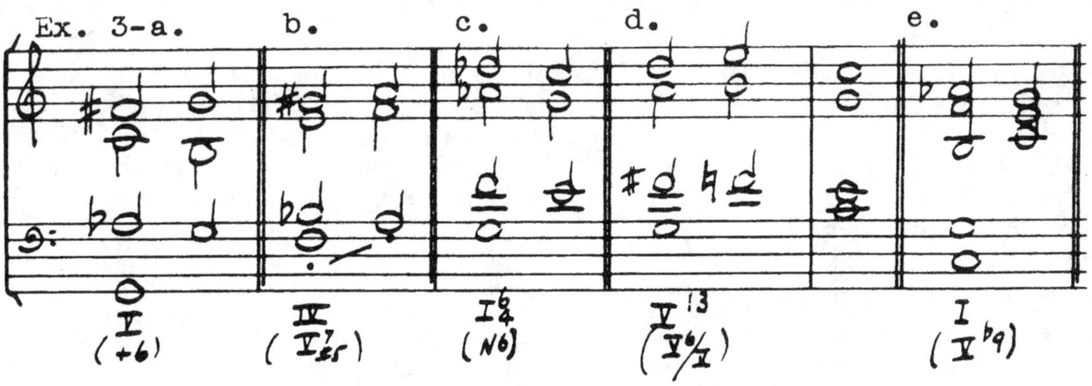

In Ex. 3 we have mixed chords based upon the augmented sixth, the neighbor dominant seventh with raised fifth, the Neapolitan sixth and the neighbor dominant of V. In Ex. 3-d the raised fourth resolves, as in many other cases, *down* into the seventh of V_7. In five-part writing mixed chords derived from major and minor ninths are of frequent occurrence, Ex. 3-e.

4 **Melodic spelling of chords.** The analysis of romantic and modern music is greatly facilitated by keeping in mind the fact that even the most "harmonic" composers were more concerned with the horizontal melodic activity of chord tones than with the vertical spelling of individual chords. As a result there are many chords which appear to be mis-spelled. Wagner supplies us with numerous examples, of which the opening bars of the Prelude to "Tristan" will suffice for illustration, Ex. 4.

Ex. 4-a

The chord in the second full measureis probably an augmented six-four-three of A minor, the G sharp in the upper part being a long sustained and accented neighbor tone. However *in sound* the chord is half-diminished, and would be correctly spelled with E sharp in the bass, a spelling which would be unmelodic, since the bass descends. It is interesting to note, never-the-less, that Wagner spells the alto part D sharp-D natural instead of the melodically logical E flat-D, which suggests that he thought of D sharp as a leading tone which falls back without achieving its resolution, and lends some support to the theory that the first of the two chords is a much altered dominant of the dominant.

In Ex. 4-b we have another half-diminished chord in sound. The spelling C-D-F-G sharp is not reducible to any chord built by thirds. The G sharp may be considered the enharmonic equivalent of A flat, or the chord may be thought of as a mixed chord, basically C-E-G sharp, the E being replaced by two neighbor tones, D and F, both emphasized and prolonged for expressive purposes. Frequently the sound and function are both clear, but the spelling is *melodic* and not harmonic, Ex. 4-c. The chord at the beginning of the second measure is obviously an augmented sixth with doubly augmented fourth, the bass G being a "simplified spelling" for A double flat. Recognition of these substitutions will greatly simplify the analysis of much chromatic music.

5 **The Pedal Point.** The stationary or pivot tone between the two chords in Examples 1 and 2 is a rudimentary form of organ or pedal point, (so called from the facility with which tones are sustained for any desired length of time by the organ pedal). In classical practice the term pedal point was used to describe a passage, written over a sustained or repeated bass tone, usually the dominant or tonic, Ex. 5 and 6.

Ex. 5. Beethoven: Sonata, Op. 28

Ex. 6. Mendelssohn: Variations sérieuses

A pedal point nearly always begins and ends with a chord of which the pedal tone forms a part; as a rule, at least half of the remaining chords will also contain the pedal tone as a chord tone, though suspensions and other non-chord tones may be involved. To the other parts the general rules of good part writing always apply; harmonically they form simple and logical progressions of clearly recognizable chords, usually complete, though in the case of seventh chords the pedal tone may replace one of the chord tones, usually the fifth.

A pedal point may occur in any of the upper voices, in which case it is termed an *inverted pedal,* Ex. 7.

Ex. 7. Chopin: Prelude No. 15

A double pedal on both tonic and dominant is of frequent occurrence; this is sometimes called a "musette bass" from the old French instrument of the bagpipe family which had a drone bass sounding these two notes, Ex. 8. Of course any scale tone may be made into a pedal point; however, if the texture is dissonant and active to any degree, the pedal tone, through the mere fact of its reiteration, tends to assume the importance of a tonic. The longer it is sustained or repeated, the more it tends to establish itself as the principal tone, subordinating all others to it.

Ex. 8.

EXERCISES, GROUP I Mixed Chords

4.

GROUP II Pedal Point

(Add inner parts)

5

6.

7.

8.

CHAPTER XXIX

HARMONIZATION OF FLORID MELODIES

1 The free application of non-chord tones to a melodic line produces what may be termed a florid or embellished melody. The embellishments are usually an inherent part of the melody itself, and not merely incidental ornaments, and they provide both color and active propulsive force through the placing of dissonances upon strong rhythmic points.

Harmonization of melodies of this type provides practice in discriminating between chord and non-chord tones, and since the style is instrumental rather than vocal, opportunity is also afforded for the devising of simple accompaniment figures. The first step is to determine which tones are chord tones and which are non-chord tones, to mark the latter with the proper signs, and to indicate with complete figuring the chord structure against which these non-chord tones are to be heard. This will require careful thought, as frequently several possibilities of by no means equal value may be found.

2 **Selection and Placement of Chords.** It may be stated as axiomatic that *the more elaborate the melody, the simpler the harmonic background.* Of course it is possible to sound non-chord tones against a complex chromatic chord structure; the exercises for the present chapter, however, have been designed in such a way that a comparatively simple harmonization will suffice, though this does not by any means exclude the use of some chromatic and altered chords. The principles of *harmonic rhythm* must be constantly kept in mind. (Review Chapter XII, Sec. 4, p. 49) The harmonic changes should appear natural and unforced, with particular care to avoid syncopated changes, unless these form part of a well defined pattern. A few illustrations will help to make this clear.

Ex. 1. The occurrence of G and E on the second and third beats respectively of measure one may cause a careless student to assume a change from I to V on the second beat, which not only produces an awkward syncopation, but also makes a regressive progression into the obvious harmony of the second measure.

Ex. 1

Ex. 2. The second measure could be harmonized with V9, but since the third measure must also be dominant, the result is a dull harmonic repetition, and in addition the notes on the first and third beats are much more expressive if heard as neighbor tones against subdominant or supertonic harmony, which fills out the simple harmonic formula: I - IV - V - I.

Ex. 2

Ex. 3. The *compound neighbor group* is a cause of frequent miscalculation. The C on the second beat is obviously a chord tone, as it is rhythmically too strong to be a neighbor tone left by a leap. The second measure could be harmonized either with II or V; depending on what follows.

Ex. 3

Ex. 4. The actual chord tones in a melody are often of much shorter duration than the neighbor tones, which should not be misinterpreted as chord tones merely because they are sustained. Their expressive energy is entirely dissipated by chords which include them as harmonic tones.

Ex. 4

3 **Accompaniment figures.** The presentation of harmonic patterns through the medium of the pianoforte involves many problems caused by the sustaining pedal, the use of arpeggio figures, "broken chords" and many other devices. The more elaborate forms of piano music are beyond the scope of the present volume, but simple accompaniment figures can be devised with little difficulty.

Ex. 5. Chopin: Prelude in E minor

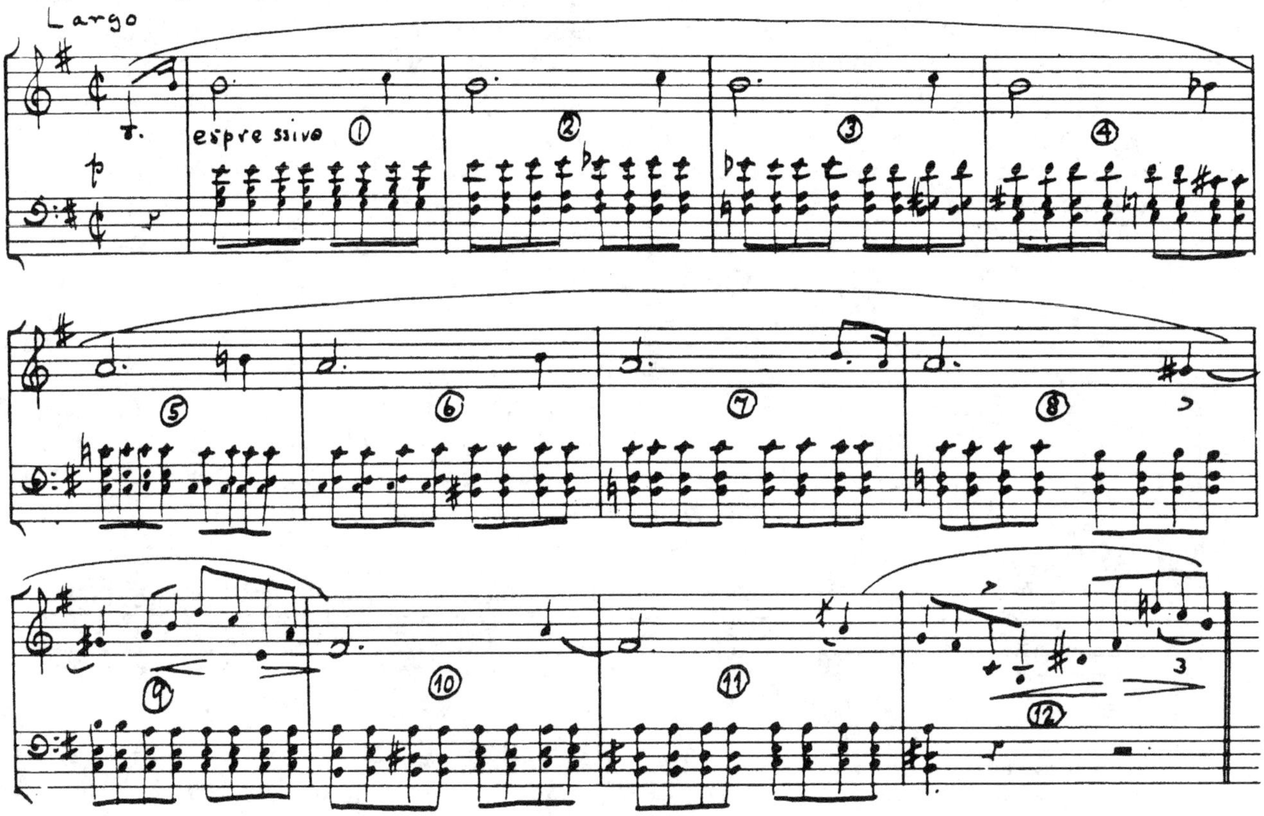

Sometimes the four-part harmony is retained intact, the impression of sustained chords being given by quiet repetition of the lower tones combined with the use of the sustaining pedal, as in the well-known Chopin Prelude, Ex. 5. The lower three parts must obviously be kept close enough together to be conveniently played with the left hand.

Ex. 6. Russian Folk Tune

The Russian Folk Tune, Ex. 6, illustrates the same treatment, with livelier rhythmic effect.

Ex. 7. Waltz

Figures of the familiar waltz type, Ex. 7 and 8, are particularly easy and useful for the student whose piano technic is limited. The following comments should be carefully studied:

a) A bass tone on an accent functions as the true bass for the succeeding figuration until the next accented bass tone is heard. Thus there is no six-four chord in the second measure of Ex. 7.

b) Common tones should be kept, as far as practicable, in the same relative position in successive figures. The left hand part of Ex. 7 could readily be converted into a sustained accompaniment for organ or male quartet without changing a note except in the next to the last measure. Here, for obvious rhythmic reasons, the II and the V chords have to be compressed into the same measure, and the right hand supplies the missing 3rd and 5th in the left hand V_7 chord.

c) Except in figures on the dominant harmony, the first tone sounded above the root (in fundamental triads) should be the fifth or octave, and almost never the third, which sounds thick and heavy, Ex. 7-b.

d) An accompanimental figure or pattern should be maintained with as few changes as possible. Patterns alternating root triads and first inversions are common, Ex. 8; here the characteristic embellishment in the figure occurs on the fifth of root triads and the root of first inversions. Note that the figure is almost always abandoned in the cadence measure.

e) If more than four parts are present or implied, the rules of four-part doubling do not apply. Care should be used, however, to see that doubling of major thirds, especially if they are leading tones, does not produce awkward effects. The sounding of neighbor tones against their resolutions is common, but some discrimination must be used to avoid thickness or blurring. If the dissonance in a melodic part is sounded by a different timbre, such as voice or violin, it is much less pronounced than when all the parts are sounded on the same instrument. In general it may be said that chromatic neighbors should not be doubled, and that it is better to avoid sounding them against their resolutions whenever possible.

FLORID MELODIES

1. Waltz

2. Slow

3. Vigorous

4. Fast

5. Waltz

6. Moderate

7. Flowing

8. Lively

9. Fast

10. Flowing

11. Slow

12. Moderate

CHAPTER XXX

HARMONY IN FIVE OR MORE PARTS

1 A large amount of music, both choral and instrumental, employs harmonic combinations of five or more different tones sounded together. The addition of a fifth tone to a chord requires the doubling of two tones of a triad, and one of a seventh chord; however it permits ninth chords to be presented complete, and makes available a large number of eleventh and thirteenth chords, as well as practically endless combinations of mixed chords.

The following example from J. S. Bach illustrates some of the possibilities, including an aggressive use of dissonance not usually associated with the music of the eighteenth century. Indeed, if some of the chords, such as those marked with an asterisk, were lifted from their context, they could be inserted in a "modern" score and find themselves perfectly at home! Particularly interesting is Bach's use of cross relations in the second measure; on the first beat major and minor sevenths are heard in direct succession, and on the third beat he anticipates the much used modern device of sounding major and minor thirds so that they are heard as forming part of the same chord.

Ex. 1. J. S. Bach: Kyrie, Gott Heiliger Geist

2 **Doubling.** In diatonic five-part writing some questions of doubling are involved. In triads it is possible to triple the root, especially in final chords, but the part writing is usually facilitated by doubling fifths and thirds, which may be done much more freely than in four-part writing, Ex. 2.

Seventh chords may double any tone; the least good tones to double are the seventh and the third, especially if the latter is a leading tone, since only one of the doubled tones will be able to resolve normally, and the other will have to progress in a manner contrary to its usual tendency. Even this may be managed, however, if no serious contrapuntal defect ensues, Ex. 3.

With regard to consecutives, an occasional parallel fifth may occur, as well as fifths by contrary motion; parallel octaves, which reduce the score to four real parts, should be avoided. Ex. 4.

Ex. 2 Ex. 3 Ex. 4

3 **Chromatic tones,** which add color without doubling tones already present in other voices are easily handled in five parts, and produce many interesting combinations not available in four parts, Ex. 5. Note, in measure 1, an incomplete dominant thirteenth, figured 7-4-3 ; in measures 3 and 4, mixed chords resolving in the second half of the measure.

Ex. 5

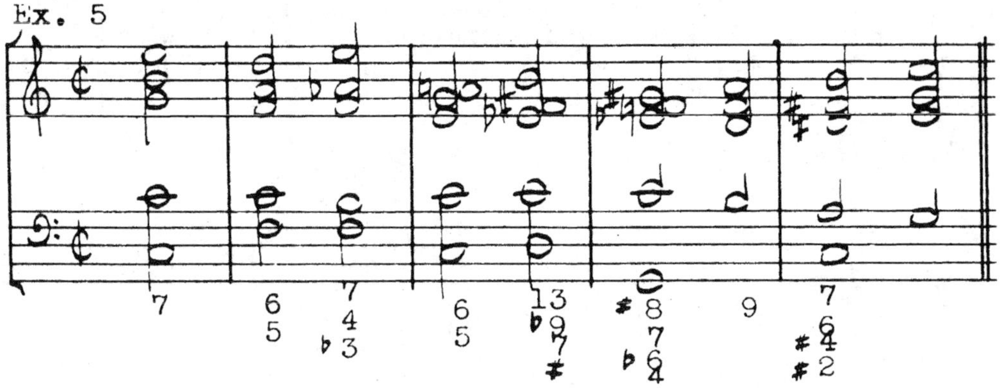

4 **Chords of the dominant eleventh,** to which brief reference was made in Chapter XV, p. 58 , become increasingly available in five-part writing, especially with one or more chromatic alterations. The unaltered form, Ex. 6-a, usually omits the leading tone to avoid sounding it against the eleventh which is the octave of its resolution. This is not strictly a dominant chord, since the omission of the third leaves a chord undefined with regard to major-minor quality. If the eleventh is raised, Ex. 6-b, the conflict between leading tone and resolution disappears; in fact this form is similar in sound to the dominant ninth with lowered fifth. Ex. 6-c shows a mixed chord which appears to be a derivative of the eleventh chord. Note that the *augmented octave,* (enharmonic of the minor ninth) frequently appears in five-part chords, (see also Ex. 5, meas. 3.)

Ex. 6-a. b. c.

5 **Degrees of dissonance.** Chromatic writing of this type produces many examples of deferred resolution, that is, passing from one discord combination to another. The ultimate result is a texture consisting entirely of dissonant combinations. We have used the term "mixed chord" to describe those chords not reducible to a position in which its members form a series of superimposed thirds

above a root. This term describes a stage in the historical evolution of harmony, in which the more dissonant elements were looked upon as accessories, of a "non-harmonic" type. When the point is reached where these dissonant elements no longer "resolve" they can hardly be called neighbor tones, and it becomes necessary to consider such chords as independent units making free use of any of the twelve chromatic tones of the scale. The lack of root feeling in most chords of this kind throws special emphasis on the voice leading of the parts, which must be handled with meticulous care.

It is obvious that tonal feeling, the basis of classical form, is very easily destroyed by this process, so that some other means of formal integration must be devised to replace it. The most successful modern music seems to employ rather carefully differentiated *degrees of dissonance,* producing an ebb and flow of harmonic tension which can be most effective. It is difficult to establish arbitrary rules for the measurement of degrees of dissonance, though such a system is presented by Hindemith in his "Craft of Musical Composition". The general classification will proceed through six stages as follows: 1. concords only; 2. soft discords; 3. the tritone; 4. combination of tritone with soft discords; 5. hard discords; 6. combination of soft and hard discords with tritone. ("soft" discords: augmented fifth, minor seventh, major second; "hard" discords, major seventh, minor second.)

Ex. 7 Degrees of Dissonance

In the stages illustrated above the dissonances are presented in their order of harmonic value, (see Chapter II, Sec. 5, p. 10 .), first singly and then in combination. Obviously many further combinations are possible, such as adding an augmented fifth (G sharp) in stage 5-a, but these merely produce subdivisions without displacing the combination in relation to those that precede and follow.

The chords illustrated above are all reducible to root chords erected in thirds. Mixed chords, however, containing elements not so reducible, are equally common in modern music, and sometimes form a large part of its texture. Chords such as the following occur with great frequency:

Ex. 8

The degree of dissonance is indicated by the number above each chord. The "mixed" chords will probably be heard as slightly more dissonant than the "unmixed" chords in the same category. Combinations with both major and minor thirds are frequent, and the amount of dissonance in stage six can be built up to any desired extent.

6 In some of these chords the root or fundamental tone is obvious; in others it is vague. The presence of a *perfect fifth* (or its inversion, the perfect fourth) in any chord, not matter how many chromatic tones may be superimposed upon it, tends strongly to establish its lower tone as the fundamental of the whole sound-complex. Lacking a perfect fifth, those combinations of major seconds and thirds and minor sixths and sevenths which make up the familiar dominant seventh chord and its first and third inversions (the second inversion contains a perfect fourth) have a strong root feeling.

Definite root feeling is vague if the above elements are lacking. Chords with obvious roots assist in establishing tonal feeling; those without tend to give the effect of embellishing chords, in which the most important considerations are the degree of dissonance and especially the melodic and contrapuntal interest involved. Ex. 9 illustrates some very common procedures of this kind, which should prove readily analyzable according to the foregoing principles.

Ex. 9

7 **Modern harmonic devices.** The student who has mastered the principles of harmonic procedure outlined in the preceding chapters will have no great difficulty in making a satisfactory analysis of any tonal music. The so-called "atonal" system, or "twelve tone technique", which is a highly specialized method of construction, has been admirably described by Ernst Krenek in his "Modern Counterpoint" (G. Schirmer, N. Y.) to which the student is referred for further information.

Many textbooks give the impression that although "traditional" harmony is easily within the grasp of the average student, a vast chasm exists between it and "modern" harmony, which is represented as being full of esoteric and ineluctable mysteries. Detailed description stops with the late romantic period, inferring that from 1900 on harmonic practice followed no set plan, adhered to no discoverable rules, and was dictated purely by the whim of the composer.

A complete analysis of all the devices used more or less successfully by twentieth century composers in the effort to achieve harmonic originality is hardly within the scope of this book, but an examination of characteristic samples will reveal the fact that all intelligible music is constructed in accordance with some recognizable system which yields its secrets to careful analysis; that the majority of the devices used show some continuity with the established practices of the past; and that they are all inevitably based upon the physical laws of sound which are as immutable as the law of gravity. Some of the more common procedures may be classified as follows:

(1) *The use of modal and other unusual scales.* This is a process of selection, omitting a great many chromatic tones, and usually produces a very simple harmonic texture.

(2) *The use of chords in parallel motion,* following the procedure of ancient *organum.* Since the principles of tonality are based upon the precise use of chords of varying intervallic structure, the result is a vagueness of tonal feeling which easily becomes "atonal" if other means of tonal unity are not employed.

(3) *The use of the whole-tone scale* and chords based upon it. As these chords contain neither perfect fifth nor fourth, tonal feeling is almost wholly absent, except that which is suggested by constant repetition of a tone or tones. The monotonous result cause this device to be largely abandoned, even by its principal protagonist, Claude Debussy, in his more mature works.

(4) *The use of chords in parallel motion against other parts moving by contrary motion.* This is an extension of the mixed chord principle, frequently employed in the late nineteenth century by such composers as Franck, and produces many interesting effects.

(5) *The use of the pedal point, or pedal chord,* sustained through a texture into which almost any dissonant combinations may be introduced without disturbing tonal feeling.

(6) *Mixed or combination chords* which result from an extension of the classical devices of suspension and anticipation, in which parts of certain chords are heard against parts of others as a result of a process of contrapuntal "dislocation". This device can also be traced well back into the nineteenth century.

(7) *Modern contrapuntal treatment* which emphasizes an interesting variety of the twelve chromatic tones in the melodic lines, with little regard for the incidental harmonic combinations produced. Banal and obvious chords and progressions are intentionally avoided; major-minor feeling is frequently nullified by sounding both major and minor thirds or by omitting the third altogether. In the most successful examples a considerable number of chords containing perfect fifths or fourths are heard, so arranged as to support some tonal feeling.

The early twentieth century was a period of disruption and revolt against the traditional past, and of intensive exploration along many different lines. Some of these experiments proved of little value, but out of others have come many beautiful and novel effects, which greatly enrich the resources of the contemporary composer. As in all other arts, time is the factor of ultimate decision in the survival of those harmonic procedures which have permanent value.

Exercises. Extensive experimentation with modern harmonic devices is so closely bound up with the study of composition that it is quite beyond the scope of the present volume. For the sake of the student who wishes to make further acquaintance with some of the possibilities, a few exercises are appended, chiefly in the hope that they will provide a starting point for more extended studies, which can here be only hinted at.

The first two exercises are to be done in five parts, and contain only diatonic tones of the seven-tone scale. Exercise 3, also in five parts, is opulently chromatic, but based mostly upon the principle of mixed chords which resolve to simple consonances.

From Exercise 4 on, the twelve chromatic tones of the scale are used independently, although the treatment varies considerably. Exercise 4 is to be done in four parts, and to be harmonized *exclusively* with major or minor triads, root position or inverted; except for the first pair of chords and the last pair, however, *no two successive chords belong to the same key.*

Exercise 5, to be done in five parts, utilizes progressions in parallel fourths; the right hand part of the first two phrases is mostly parallel six-four chords; in the third and fourth phrases, seven-four chords.

Exercises 6, 7 and 8 make free use of the twelve tone scale, and may be worked in three, four or five parts, the simpler versions being usually the best. The student should indicate the *degrees of dissonance,* in these latter exercises, and try to work out an interesting and varied treatment of this important factor.

EXERCISES

5. Flowing

6. Slow

7. Energetic

8. Lively, with vigor